COLLECTOR'S EDITION

Entertainment
WEEKLY

THE ULTIMATE GUIDE TO

Justice League

Contents

Inside

the Film

From left: Jason Momoa as Aquaman, Gal Gadot as Wonder Woman, Ezra Miller as the Flash and Ray Fisher as Cyborg as key allies ready to fight together.

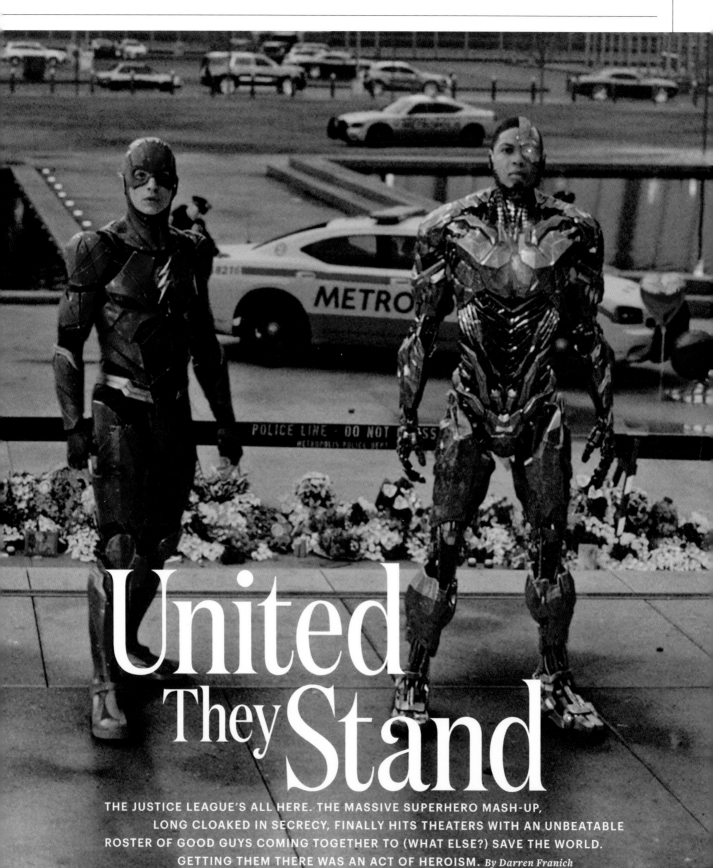

United They Stand

THE JUSTICE LEAGUE'S ALL HERE. THE MASSIVE SUPERHERO MASH-UP,
LONG CLOAKED IN SECRECY, FINALLY HITS THEATERS WITH AN UNBEATABLE
ROSTER OF GOOD GUYS COMING TOGETHER TO (WHAT ELSE?) SAVE THE WORLD.
GETTING THEM THERE WAS AN ACT OF HEROISM. *By Darren Franich*

E

EZRA MILLER RECALLS THE EXCITEMENT OF the early days of *Justice League.* The young actor had made an indie-fabulous name off attention-getting turns in *We Need to Talk About Kevin* and *The Perks of Being a Wallflower.* Then Zack Snyder, the director of 2013's *Man of Steel,* tapped Miller for *Justice.*

"All the initial conversations that I had with Zack Snyder were so mind-blowing," Miller says now. "It's hard to fathom how much work and thought that dude puts into everything he does. A lot of those conversations took place over the 4-in.-thick leather-bound books in which Zack Snyder illustrates every frame of every movie he shoots, some of them in vivid detail."

Miller (Barry Allen, better known as the Flash) wasn't merely being cast in a film. He was joining a universe at a moment of aggressive expansion. Snyder initially cast Miller for a short cameo in *Batman v Superman: Dawn of Justice.* Miller was among many new faces the director assembled for his massive superhero brawl. Say what you will, but *Batman v Superman* was very, very big—pitting Henry Cavill's tall Superman against Ben Affleck's equally tall Batman. And the titular titan clash was just the warm-up: It didn't encompass the fiery arrival of Gal Gadot's Wonder Woman.

As box office receipts for *Batman v Superman* skyrocketed last spring, Snyder went into production on *Justice League,* a successor film that would unite Gadot and Affleck with Miller and fellow franchise newbies Ray Fisher (as Cyborg) and Jason Momoa (as Aquaman). What could go wrong?

"It sold a lot of tickets," says Affleck now. "It did what it was intended to do." He's being modest—the movie grossed $873 million globally—but that modesty speaks to the mixed reactions the film inspired. "Some people liked it; some people bashed it," the Oscar-winning star admits. "It's always a little thorny playing with characters the audience already knows. You're sticking your neck out a little with movies like this."

True. Affleck's Batman reappeared in last year's *Suicide Squad,* another film that earned big money—and polarized audiences. But this summer Gadot's Diana took center stage in *Wonder Woman,* which critics and moviegoers universally adored and has sparked serious Oscar talk.

"I'm so happy to see the success of the franchise through Gal and through *Wonder Woman,*" says Amy Adams, who helped kick-start this whole mega-universe as Lois Lane in 2013's *Man of Steel.* The perennial Oscar nominee is back in *Justice League,* but don't ask her what the movie's about. "When I watch it, I'm going to find out," she says with a laugh, admitting that she only got the script pages for her scenes. "I'm happy to be a supporting player in all of this."

In *Justice League,* everyone's a supporting player. It begins with Batman's uniting Earth's superheroes in the face of a villainous cosmic force. "I wanted Bruce Wayne to build the Justice League," Snyder told *EW* in 2016, "having to go out and find these seven samurai by himself." He's been successful. To defend Earth from a

▲

In *Justice League*
Ben Affleck's Batman
goes recruiting.
Left: speaking to Jason
Momoa's Aquaman.
Above: with Ezra Miller's
the Flash.

◄

J.K. Simmons takes
on the role of
Commissioner Gordon
(signaling for Batman).

cosmic threat, Affleck says, his Batman brings the heroes "to the Batcave and lets them in on the central conflict of the story: who the enemy is. There's a little bit of *The Magnificent Seven* aspect to it."

Justice League is a different kind of film from its moody predecessor. Veteran producer Charles Roven, who's been working with DC heroes since 2005's *Batman Begins*, views the process of crafting *Justice League* as a healthy evolution from the reaction to *Batman v Superman*. "We were heading down a particular creative path, but it definitely made us look at some of the aspects of that path," he says.

"The idea was always that this would be a lighter movie with a lighter tone," says Affleck. That means a new dynamic between Batman and Wonder Woman. "They've got a little bit of an unusual romantic tension between them," Affleck says. Meanwhile, recruits Cyborg and the Flash must learn how to navigate a superheroic world that is decidedly new to them. "They're the youngest members of the group," explains Fisher, who plays Cyborg, "and they're the only members of the Justice League who have gotten their powers via the results of accidents."

Fisher's the freshest newcomer, with just a couple IMDB credits and a well-received onstage turn as Muhammad Ali before his casting. Cyborg's also probably the least iconic League hero (unless you're young enough to have watched the *Teen Titans* cartoon). The Flash is more familiar to audiences; Grant Gustin plays Barry Allen on the eponymous CW show. For Miller, there's something unique about the film's ability to throw so many heroes together. "I love so much about the superhero-team framework," Miller says. "It disrupts this romance surrounding individual heroism. No one can do everything, but everyone can do something."

That team framework was on display at Comic-Con International in July when the cast assembled for a high-energy panel. At one point the ever-boisterous Momoa threw his chair, then picked it up and threw it again. But offstage new difficulties were arising. Just the day before the panel,

a story from *The Hollywood Reporter* claimed Warner Bros. was planning to wind down Affleck's tenure as Batman after *Justice League*. At the time, Snyder had departed from the project because of a family tragedy—which meant he already wasn't present for what turned out to be the summer's extensive reshoots.

About those reshoots: "Zack decided that he wanted to do some additional photography," clarifies Roven. For help Snyder reached out to a director-creator beloved by the Comic-Con crowd: Joss Whedon, late of the Marvel Cinematic Universe, who was recently announced as the writer-director of the upcoming *Batgirl* film. "He thought that Joss's sensibility might be exactly right for what he was looking to do. So he showed Joss the film, and he

▲
Left: Jeremy Irons as Bruce Wayne's faithful butler (and Batman's technologically savvy partner). Above: Wonder Woman (Gal Gadot) as her alter ego, Diana Prince.

◀
It's the second time audiences will see Joe Morton, right, as Dr. Silas Stone (in S.T.A.R. Labs). He and Victor Stone made cameos in *Batman v Superman*.

talked about a number of scenes that we would be adding or expanding upon, and Joss wrote those scenes." When Snyder decided to take a step back from the project, Roven explains, he chose his collaborator as his replacement. "He asked Joss if he would do it, and Joss said yes."

Despite his late arrival in the film's production, Whedon does now carry an official cowriting credit alongside *Batman v Superman*'s Chris Terrio, a rare credit to be given this late in a movie's creation. The directorial arrangement constituted its own offscreen team-up. "They were very complementary," Affleck says. "Zack's so good with the mythic, Gothic, heavy, serious stuff, and Joss is so good with tone and comedy and making superheroes seem kind of real and relatable."

The superteam has been mythic and comedic at various points since its beginning in 1960. But the film bears a strong resemblance to the rebooted League that first appeared in 2011, when it united to face down Darkseid, a monstrous villain from planet Apokolips. Notably the plot of the movie turns on the presence of the Mother Boxes, technology tied to Apokolips.

The 2011 storyline was scripted by Geoff Johns, now the cochair of DC Films. Johns describes *Justice League* as "the center of the DC universe, where all the different worlds and characters collide. When you toss in Jack Kirby's amazing tapestry, the New Gods that he created for DC, that's such a massive backdrop with so many iconic stories." Roven explained that part of the story line began with a question. "What might happen if you're able to mix the Apokoliptan technology and the Kryptonian technology?" he asks. "What can you get then?"

Speaking of Kryptonian technology: Henry Cavill is in *Justice League*. After keeping it quiet for months (*Variety* reported this summer's reshoots were affected by the facial hair the star grew for the filming of Paramount's *Mission: Impossible 6*), Cavill came on record to *EW* to say, "It is no secret that I will be suited and booted (and caped) for *Justice League* at

some point. What is the League without our big boy blue after all?"

More solo films loom on the horizon. *Aquaman* will arrive in 2018, and Gadot will return with a *Wonder Woman* sequel the following year. Plans are in place for the Flash film, but Affleck's future in the cowl remains uncertain. For now the focus is on the union of all these characters onscreen—and the actors bringing the iconic team to life.

"We've got a pretty dope group of people," Fisher says. "From Ben, who's a little more reserved, to Jason, who breaks chairs. Ezra's just a bundle of joy and laughter. And Gal is just the sweetest, most compassionate person I know. It's really the most eclectic family of individuals you can ever imagine." Just a typical big family solving problems as big as an extended universe.

▲
Left: Queen Hippolyta
(Connie Nielsen)
and the Amazons are
back—this time
protecting their isle
from an alien threat.
Above: Amy Adams's
bereft Lois Lane.

◄
The underwater
kingdom of Atlantis is
home to Momoa's
Aquaman and Amber
Heard's Mera.

▲
Cyborg is locked and loaded (left). Right: Batman in action.

◄
Left: The Flash readies for a fight. It's a new thing for him; in the trailer, he quips, "I've never done battle. I've just pushed some people and run away." Right: Batman takes flight.

JUSTICE LEAGUE GETS CANDID

In these rare behind-the-scenes shots, we catch glimpses of the superfriends with director Zack Snyder on the set of the year's most epic hero mash-up. **BY NICOLE SPERLING**

MEETING THE FLASH

When Bruce Wayne breaks into Barry Allen's hideout, he's expecting to recruit a superhero. But when Ben Affleck first met Ezra Miller, he didn't know what to expect. "Ezra came from the most improvisational [place], funny, light," Affleck says. "Batman's definitely the darkest, most serious, most somber of the heroes. It was a lot of fun for me, because I got to play sort of the straight man to him. Batman's a great straight man."

TAKING THE LEAD

Gal Gadot describes Wonder Woman's relationship with Bruce Wayne as tolerant co-parents. "They are the mature ones, the adults of the team," she says. Offscreen that meant the superpowered duo took the leadership roles when director Zack Snyder relinquished control of his film to writer/director Joss Whedon after a family tragedy. (Whedon was responsible for the writing and directing of the new scenes shot during the six weeks of reshoots, though Snyder remains the only credited director.) What was that experience like? Says Gadot: "It's been different. It's the first time I've been working on a film starting with one director and finishing with a different one. It's been an interesting experience. A positive experience."

UNDER HER EYE

Not only is Wonder Woman responsible for saving mankind, she also felt the need to boost the morale of the members of her league, specifically the younger ones like Cyborg and the Flash. "She feels responsible for them in a way," Gadot says. "She's been fighting for so many years, so many decades, but all of a sudden she has these newcomers, and some of them are teenagers. She's very protective of them."

ROCK AND ROLL HERO

Sitting atop the Batmobile, adorned in 40 lbs. of Aquaman armor, Jason Momoa's Arthur Curry may just be expanding his fiefdom from the sea onto land. Or he's just continuing the prankster relationship he shares with the Dark Knight. "He's just Batman," says Momoa of his relationship with Bruce Wayne. "He's like my older brother. I'm kind of a ballbuster toward him." Momoa looked to an unlikely source for inspiration when creating this larger than life superhero—Guns N' Roses guitarist Slash: "He's my spirit animal," he says. "When I'm walking down that runway, I'm singing 'Rocket Queen' in my head. Slash is a beast." And so, it seems, is Aquaman.

Left to right:
Jason Momoa,
Ben Affleck,
Gal Gadot,
Ray Fisher, and
Ezra Miller.

the
CAST TALKS
to EW!

ROLE MODELS

On-set bromances, the (inevitable) sequels and spinoffs, the difficulties of portraying a superhero: The stars of *Justice League* break their silence.
BY DARREN FRANICH AND NICOLE SPERLING

BATMAN Ben Affleck

○ Batman's cool, right? The cape, the mask, the car, the chin? But after two films behind the cowl—not to mention a cameo in *Suicide Squad*—Ben Affleck's discovered the Dark Knight's biggest secret. "Playing Bruce Wayne is the most fun," the actor says. "The director almost plays Batman. The director sets up the dynamic and the look, the feel, the sound, the fights. All that stuff is pre-rigged. It's Bruce Wayne where you can be a little more free." And in *Justice League,* he does feel free, letting go of the rage that powered his enmity with the Kryptonian hero across the river. "In [*Batman v Superman: Dawn of Justice*], he was kind of confused, harboring all this anger and resentment toward Superman. He kind of became blind," Affleck says.

That attitude doesn't work when you're assembling a team of heroes to save the world. "He's got to overcome his misanthropic tendencies. He's kind of a loner. He has to get past that." For the actor, the team-up film was a chance to explore Bruce's relationship with other characters, to "play the dynamics, the sexual tension with Wonder Woman, the regular old tension with Flash." What about Aquaman? "You can't be around Jason Momoa and not have sexual tension," Affleck admits. All too true.

The Cast

WONDER WOMAN Gal Gadot

○ Gal Gadot might have reigned as the queen of the box office this summer, but that doesn't mean her big-screen alter ego doesn't have obstacles to overcome when she returns to action in *Justice League*. For one, loneliness still plagues Wonder Woman. The demigod also known as Princess Diana left her home of Themyscira to save mankind only to lose the love of her life, Steve Trevor, to an act of heroism. Now she is back, trying to unite a team of misfits again to save the world. "She is still lonely. She does still feel like an outsider," Gadot says. "But my point from the get-go [on *Justice League*] was I thought Wonder Woman should be the glue. She should be the emotional support. The fact that each and every member of the team is an outcast and an outsider, it almost feels like she's found a new family."

To ensure that connection, Gadot's priority was making the most of moments in which Wonder Woman bonds with each member of the team. Gadot says Diana boosts Flash's confidence, diminishes Cyborg's feeling of isolation, connects with Aquaman over their superhero status and engages in a little co-parenting with Bruce Wayne.

She's also got the future to think about. Now that *Wonder Woman* director Patty Jenkins has signed on for the sequel, Gadot can focus on where she will take her iconic character next. "We had so much work to do in the first one. We had to establish the character, [tell] the complete origin story," she says. "Now we have leverage. We can show how she's doing in a man's world. [It can be] fun, funny—and dramatic. And I can't wait to start shooting it." We can't wait to see it.

AQUAMAN Jason Momoa

○ There are few actors as aligned with their onscreen personas as Jason Momoa is with Aquaman. These two share their stranger-in-two-land status—Momoa is from Hawaii and raised in Iowa; superhero Arthur Curry occupies both Atlantis and the world above the sea. Momoa's extensive tattoos were even the starting inspiration for his Aquaman costume. (When on-set, you could often find him huddled together with costumer designer Michael Wilkinson.) And don't get him started on the jewelry: Most of the rings, necklaces and other accoutrements that adorn the Aquaman costume came from Momoa's "many Airstreams of junk" that he's personally collected over the years. "I guess if I could be a superhero, Aquaman is pretty dead-on," he says.

While the 38-year-old is now deeply immersed in exploring the hero for his upcoming stand-alone movie, due out next year, in *Justice League* the strapping underwater adventurer is a reluctant team player. "You'll get to see the ballbuster. He's pretty gruff, he's very sarcastic, and he's a bit of a loner," Momoa says. "But he has to get over his own little problems and join the team because it's really not about him."

And Momoa, for one, can't wait to see the finished product. "It's the perfect time for this thing to come out," he says. "You couldn't shoot Aquaman before. You couldn't shoot him underwater. Now with the visual effects, it's going to be pretty exciting."

THE FLASH Ezra Miller

○ What role does rookie hero Barry Allen serve in the high-powered League, with its billionaire and its immortal princess and its undersea King? "He's a great intern," jokes actor Ezra Miller. "He can get coffee so fricking quickly." But, like, in combat? "We continue to ride in Batman's vehicles because they're super-fricking awesome and have rockets and stuff attached," Miller notes. "But, theoretically, the Flash is your slightly more nauseating—but free!—Uber." The actor's enthusiasm matches his character—an important point that goes all the way back to Allen's first appearance in 1956, when the character was a scientist obsessed with reading the tales of the Golden Age Flash. "Barry has a fascinated mind. He is a fan of heroes," Miller says.

Miller's training went way beyond jogging, with a trip to China to study Wudang Kung Fu. But to hear him explain it, the Flash's speed is the tip of the iceberg. "Zack [Snyder] was very interested in some of the quantum enigmas of the character, exploring the power beyond just being fast. These notions of molecular control, interdimensional travel." Of course, Miller points out that Barry is still early in his world-saving career. Maybe for now, we'll just focus on the coffee.

CYBORG Ray Fisher

○ Batman is Bruce Wayne. The Flash is Barry Allen. Cyborg is . . . complicated. "He's the only member of the League who can't take his costume off," says Ray Fisher, who debuted as Victor Stone for a limbless cameo in *Batman v Superman*. The football-star son of a brilliant scientist, Victor is left near death by an accident that decimates his body—and his family. "He's dealing with the loss of his body and also dealing with the simultaneous loss of his mother. His father, with whom he has a very strange relationship, takes it upon himself to rebuild Victor." Deadpans Fisher: "He's juggling a whole lot, man."

When *Justice League* begins, Victor's been Cyborg for about a year, living a Quasimodo-esque existence in the shadows. A higher calling to superheroism comes with the cosmic threat to Earth. For Victor, it's a personal threat too. "The technology that created him is a Mother Box, this Apokoliptian technology," Fisher says. "It calls into question himself: 'Is it possible for the machine to take me over?'" Fisher hopes to further explore Victor's trauma in the announced *Cyborg* spinoff. "You want to leave space for the characters to evolve," he explains. "I'd love to see a Cyborg stand-alone film that's a little bit more intimate."

SUPERMAN Henry Cavill

○ No question about it. At the conclusion of *Batman v Superman*, the Last Son of Krypton was dead and gone, having sacrificed himself to stop the terror-creature Doomsday. But let's be honest—it takes more than death to stop the ultimate hero. "It is no secret that I will be suited and booted (and caped) for *Justice League*," said actor Henry Cavill weeks before the movie debuted. "What is the League without our big boy blue, after all?"

Very true. Except for the fact that for a time leading up to its release it actually was one of *Justice League*'s biggest secrets. Would Superman return? And if so, how exactly? Fans mined comic-book history for clues. In a '90s story arc, Superman was resurrected via Kryptonian technology, the same alien science that Lex Luthor used to transform the neck-snapped Zod into Doomsday in Zack Snyder's last costumed crusader match-up.

Cavill says the character's demise paved the way for an intriguing *Justice League* arc. "One of the most exciting things about Superman's death in *Batman v Superman* is that it provided a wonderful springboard for a chrysalis-like event," he says.

The actor welcomed the opportunity to further complicate his incarnation of Clark Kent's superside. "Despite his renown and despite his popularity in pop culture worldwide, he has had the most difficult introduction as a character in this movie universe so far," Cavill says. "He is difficult to understand. His complexity goes far deeper than 'just doing the right thing.'"

JK Simmons as Commissioner Gordon.

TEAM PLAYERS

Every superhero has an Alfred (in Batman's case, quite literally). The cast members who round out the film discuss their ever-expanding roles.
BY DARREN FRANICH AND NICOLE SPERLING

COMMISSIONER GORDON
JK Simmons

○ When the *Whiplash* Oscar winner signed on to play the Caped Crusader's signal-shining lawman ally, he dove into the research—which meant phoning his actor friends. "I went through some of the old comics," Simmons explains, "and called a couple of buddies of mine, Corey Reynolds and Bruno Campos—major DC fanatics." His pals guided him to an important realization. "He's kind of a badass. He's kind of a tough guy. Gary Oldman did a wonderful and iconic portrayal of the Commissioner, but people also know Gordon from the original *Batman* TV show. Friendly, ineffectual, 'Oh, help, Batman!'" Simmons wanted his

Gordon to be tougher, an appropriate compatriot for Affleck's experienced hero. "You cast a 61-year-old JK Simmons, and Ben is not a twentysomething anymore, so we're obviously in a world where these two guys have a long history," the actor explains. "There's a little bit of that foxhole humor between Batman and the Commissioner."

QUEEN HIPPOLYTA
Connie Nielsen

○ When we last saw Hippolyta, she was faced with the most difficult task for an Amazon queen and a mother: saying goodbye, perhaps for good, to her beloved daughter Diana. In *Justice League*, Nielsen's

Connie Nielsen as Queen Hippolyta.

Jeremy Irons as Alfred Pennyworth.

regal leader may not be reunited with her demigoddess offspring, but she is back as the leader of the female warriors and chief custodian of a crucial artifact. With a new director and a new, much more physical mission, the 53-year-old actress found that she became stronger than ever. "Hippolyta is a really raucous and strong leader," Nielsen says. "I trained really hard for a while, and when I realized I reached a new level of strength, crested a new wave, it was truly a fantastic experience." She's not alone in those scenes, either. Hinting at the return of the Amazon warriors, Nielsen says, "you get to see Hippolyta at many different times with these costumes that are really kind of spectacular. And then you see them do battle."

ALFRED PENNYWORTH
Jeremy Irons

o Returning to play Bruce Wayne's eternally enabling butler, the Oscar-winning Irons is modest about his place in the ever-more-cosmic DC universe. "We're dealing with some amazing superheroes here," he says. "Alfred, in a way, pales in comparison. I feel very, very honored when I'm able to sit comfortably and do the crosswords, waiting for the lighting, and the guys in all their gear are sitting there pumping cold water [to keep them from overheating in] their costumes." But beyond serving as the Dark Knight's communications manager, he also fulfills an important emotional purpose in Batman's quest to unite the League. "Alfred

did raise Bruce. It's very much a father figure trying to guide his boy. He remains an ameliorating influence, trying to steady him. He's a soundboard." And although the hero quotient has increased from *Batman v Superman,* Irons describes *Justice League* as "a little bit less stuffed. I think the story is stronger." (Don't argue with Alfred; he cooks and cleans *and* has spare keys to the Batmobile!)

LOIS LANE **Amy Adams**

o The world lost Superman, but Lois Lane lost Clark Kent. And when we find the *Daily Planet*'s Pulitzer-winning investigative reporter, that loss still weighs heavily on her. "She's definitely struggling to

Amy Adams as Lois Lane.

Diane Lane as Martha Kent.

come to terms with the situation and figure out how to get past it, get redirected
back toward her spirited self," Adams says.
"She finds herself very stuck." Adams says
she was segregated from most of the rest
of the cast, shooting her story arc and
scenes in a bubble. But she shares a bond
with Diane Lane's Martha Kent, who has a
mutual loss in common. "I don't know the
universe around me," she explains. "My
story line sort of exists in parallel but
doesn't intersect too much with the larger
picture." Would she ever want Lois to
become a costumed superhero, a common
plot point in the 1950s? "I think we're
loaded with superpowers," she laughs.
"It's nice to get to use your compassion
and your brains." Hey, the pen *is* mightier
than the Kryptonite spear.

MARTHA KENT
Diane Lane

o In *Man of Steel*, she lost a husband. In
Batman v Superman, she buried her son.
"Martha's a smart woman," Lane says.
"You do have to pick up and move on. It's
overwhelming for her alone, that life she
used to live, without the support of her
spouse or son." But she's not completely
alone. "I did enjoy some additional photography with Amy [Adams]," she says.
Lane's reunion with the other woman in
the late Clark Kent's life has an impact on
the events in *Justice League*. "We had a scene
that is, I think, pivotal." The actress
declares her admiration for the character
she's played since 2013's *Man of Steel*. "I
adore Martha's pragmatism and honesty.

I find her very refreshing, compared to a
lot of intellectualizing, you know? She
trusts her gut." It took a tough woman to
raise a Superman.

DR. SILAS STONE
Joe Morton

o A father dedicated to his job, a son
desperate for attention. That's how we
meet Silas Stone and his son Victor. "Dr.
Stone is not one of those fathers who goes
to a football game to watch his son play,"
Morton says. "He's a scientist, kind of an
absentee dad." When a traumatic accident
leaves his son ravaged, his paternal
instincts kick in—though there's also a
touch of Dr. Frankenstein in his decision

Joe Morton as Dr. Silas Stone.

to use his cosmic research to transform his son into the superhero Cyborg.

"Dr. Stone puts his son back together again, and you would think his son would be very pleased to be alive," Morton says. "Cyborg has one eye, he has this mechanical arm, he has all these abilities which are frightening. In a certain kind of way, his story is about being the Other. His father keeps trying to lead him in the direction of 'Don't you see all you could do for the world, given all the abilities you have?'" It's something of a return for the actor, who played cybernetic researcher Miles Dyson in *Terminator 2: Judgment Day*. "I guess this is my reputation now," Morton says with a laugh. "I'm the guy that puts people back together, and they're not quite human!"

> **"I adore Martha's pragmatism and honesty. I find her very refreshing.... She trusts her gut"**
>
> —*Diane Lane*

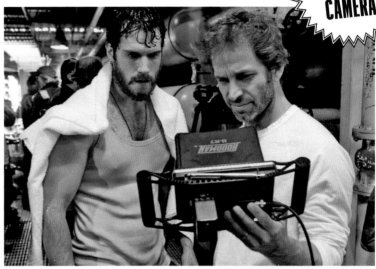

THE DIRECTOR

A family tragedy forced Zack Snyder to step away from *Justice League*. But his legacy powers the DC movieverse, merging comic-book culture with modern cinema. **BY DARREN FRANICH**

"THERE'S A MYTHOLOGICAL JOURNEY FOR Superman," Zack Snyder told *EW* in 2016. "There's the birth, death and resurrection thing." When the director spoke to the magazine, his Kryptonian hero had just reached the middle of that cycle, buried in a Kansas coffin at the end of *Batman v Superman: Dawn of Justice*. For Snyder that decision was designed to set up the high stakes for *Justice League*. "Without Superman," he explained, "there is definitely a vulnerability to the team."

The mythological and the vulnerable: Those two poles describe Snyder's approach to superhero narratives, his particular knack for hyperbolizing comic-book stories with slow-motion pageantry while also anchoring his heroes in a grimy, dirty reality. That strategy was already on display in *300*, a lavishly faithful adaptation of Frank Miller's historical adventure, at once graphically gory and almost cartoonlike in its excess.

Its success gave Snyder carte blanche. Boldly, he decided that his third feature film would be *Watchmen,* the eternally acclaimed Alan Moore/Dave Gibbons graphic novel. Snyder ratcheted up the satire, drenching the soundtrack in classic tunes. He also ratcheted up, well, everything, indulging in R-rated comic ultraviolence. "The movie is a challenge," Snyder explained in 2008, "to your icons, your morality, how you perceive pop culture, how you perceive mythology and, for that matter, how you perceive God."

That sense of godhood, both embraced and deconstructed, runs through Snyder's superhero work. Look at *Man of Steel,* in which Henry Cavill's Superman is steeped in Christ imagery—even as it builds to the shocking, morality-challenging neck-snap heard 'round the world. *Batman v Superman* was a smash-up of icons, but the film's most vivid details are tableaux: Superman surrounded by skull-masked Day of the Dead celebrants, Batman rising out of his Batmobile to face his Kryptonian frenemy. The film drew considerably from the work of Frank Miller—Affleck models the Batarmor from *The Dark Knight Returns*—and served as a culmination for a whole generation that grew up worshipping the *300* artist's grandiosity.

Justice League promises to be Snyder's most expansive endeavor, bringing in the villainous denizens of Apokolips—characters creator Jack Kirby literally called the New Gods. After stepping away under painful circumstances, his future with the franchise is unclear—he has said publicly that his superhero days might now be behind him. But the DC movies are filled with stars cast by Snyder and the aesthetic he crafted. Snyder produced and had a story credit on *Wonder Woman,* whose band of demigod female warriors could almost be seen as a triumphant, gendered rejoinder to the *300* manfest. We may have only seen the dawn of Snyder's superheroic visions.

From top: behind the scenes of *Man of Steel*: Henry Cavill and Snyder; Amy Adams and Snyder; Kevin Costner and Snyder.

THE WRITER

INSIDE ☆☆ the ☆☆ STORY

Joss Whedon's comic-book roots stretch back decades—and his previous work might point to a new future for the DC cinematic universe.
BY DARREN FRANICH

IT WAS COMIC-CON INTERNATIONAL 2013, and Joss Whedon was riding high. A year earlier his second feature film, Marvel's *The Avengers,* helped to usher in a new era of Hollywood cinematic universes. He could hold forth with some authority about tackling a comic-book adaptation. "I think a lot of directors, in some superhero movies that don't necessarily work as well," Whedon said at the time, "they have to, like, talk themselves into it. They have to say, 'Well, I guess I can find a way into this character…and then I'll try to translate it.' But for me, that step is eliminated. That's a second language to me."

It's true that few people speak comic book as effortlessly and as fluently as the creator of *Buffy the Vampire Slayer,* which featured Sarah Michelle Gellar as bloodsucker-slaying superwoman struggling through a mythology worthy of Jack Kirby. Now, with his joining *Justice League* as co-writer alongside *Batman v Superman: Dawn of Justice* scribe Chris Terrio, Whedon brings a world of unique expertise (and maybe also some of his trademark funny?) to the DC superhero stable.

Famously quippy banter aside, Whedon is a master at crafting compelling ensembles and expertly dissecting group dynamics. He proved that again and again on *Buffy,* but after the cancellation of his shortlived sci-fi series *Firefly,* Whedon also put his own spin on one of his beloved comic-book franchises: X-Men. "We're a superhero team," says Cyclops in the first issue of Whedon's run. "And I think it's time we started acting like one." For the 2004-era X-Men, that meant a style change back to a traditional look, after years of *Matrix*-y jumpsuits. ("And quite frankly, all the black leather is making people nervous," says Cyclops.)

The 2000s were a black-leather phase for comic-book characters onscreen, dominated by Christopher Nolan's *Dark Knight* trilogy. Meanwhile, the somewhat sunnier Whedon drafted an unproduced *Wonder Woman* screenplay and invented an outcast bad guy who just wants to belong. Released online when YouTube was barely a thing, *Dr. Horrible's Sing-Along Blog* cast Neil Patrick Harris as a mad scientist who's also a lovesick loser desperate to join the superpowered team Evil League of Evil. His nemesis is Nathan Fillion's Captain Hammer, a publicity-hounding braggart who suggests a cockeyed take on the Superman archetype.

As the man charged with finalizing director Zack Snyder's vision, Whedon is entering a very different sort of league, and he's set to stick around the DC franchise for some time as the director of a *Batgirl* film for Warner Bros. He might be a new arrival in this universe, but he already speaks the language.

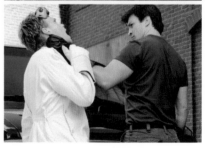

▲
From top, some of Whedon's projects: Summer Glau from *Firefly;* the Scooby gang in *Buffy the Vampire Slayer;* the stars of *Dr. Horrible's Sing-Along Blog.*

PICTURE PERFECT

Production designer Patrick Tatopoulos shares details of the film's design, including the exciting new weapons in Batman's personal armory.

BY NICOLE SPERLING AND DARREN FRANICH

BATMAN AND BEYOND

Tatopoulos became a key collaborator for director Zack Snyder on 2016's *Batman v Superman: Dawn of Justice,* developing a new look for Gotham's loner hero. "[Snyder wanted] a Batman that's tough, bold, stronger, a little older.... It felt like the guy was brutal—like Brutalism in architecture. This is why the Batcave is made of blocks; the glass house is very blocky." On *Justice League* Tatopoulos designed the hero's fleet of vehicles, and he found it exciting to create whole aesthetics around the characters. "The great thing about *Justice League* was more about: 'What is the palette for Flash's world? What is the palette for Wonder Woman's world? What about the world of Aquaman?'"

TEAM DYNAMICS

The League's battle scenes were choreographed with the movement of each superhero in mind—even those who were largely CGI. "The posture of Cyborg was extremely important," says Ray Fisher. "He's in a new body. His movements are a lot more difficult. He has to learn how to master that. Putting on that 30 lbs. [of muscle], I felt like I was in a different kind of shell. Being able to feel that weight, adjust the posture, adjust my shoulders."

UNDER FIRE

The crablike Knightcrawler is full of surprises. Batman's vehicle of choice when things get harried, the off-road vehicle can go into tunnels and climb, thanks to the spikes that adorn its legs and can protrude into walls. Add in its fire-shooting capabilities, and it's a formidable foe. With all this, the Knight Crawler is surefire scene-stealer. "We built the whole cockpit of this thing so we could shoot it with the actors," says Tatopoulos. "It's part of all the fun sequences in the film, and [I think] people are going to love it."

AMAZON NATION

The idyllic island of Themyscira is under attack—this time from the aliens of Apokolips who are searching for an important artifact the Amazons have vowed to protect. The warrior women are, naturally, willing to battle them at all costs. "There is this moment when the bad guys—who are just so giant and overwhelmingly huge—[come after us]—and you would kind of think the Amazons would back down from that. But we [don't], and there is a sequence of stunts that [we did] that were just amazing," says Connie Nielsen, who plays Queen Hippolyta in the film.

Concept Art

IN THE COCKPIT

Tatopoulos had his ah-ha design moment on the *Flying Fox* when he slid the cockpit all the way to the back of the top floor as a way to expand the view from inside and give it its unique design aesthetic. "[Sliding it all the way back] gave it a very different shape," he says. "When you look out from the cockpit, you see 120 feet in front of you." He also got to build the entire interior of the jet, constructing it out of mesh and structured steel so you can see in between all three floors. "I'm excited about this one," he adds.

TEAM TRANSPORT

Wayne Enterprises' *Flying Fox* is the pièce de résistance of Batman's arsenal. Three stories tall, it's the perfect vehicle to hold everything the Justice League could possibly need. The bottom floor is big enough to house the Batmobile and serve as the meeting place for disparate members of the team, while the second floor holds all the technology and media that keeps the thing moving. And, of course, up top sits the cockpit, large enough for Batman and friends to navigate the enormous jet fighter/cargo plane.

Heroes

ILLUSTRATION BY ANDY MACDONALD

ALL-STARS

Since its introduction in 1960, the Justice League has had hundreds of members and faced fearsome foes— but through it all, managed to protect the innocent. **BY JOHN JACKSON MILLER**

ZACK SNYDER'S *JUSTICE LEAGUE* MOVIE features a roster of DC Comics' heavy-hitters: Batman, Wonder Woman, Aquaman, the Flash and Cyborg—and maybe even Superman. But in the storied history of the League, more than 100 heroes have belonged to the group since the 1960s. For years issues began with an identifying "roll call." Among those present? A who's who of characters ranging from the familiar to the obscure. (How obscure, you ask? Try Congorilla, Bulleteer and the Scarlet Skier.)

Yet the team started small. In 1960 editor Julius Schwartz sought to introduce a supergroup in the mold of the 1940s' Justice Society of America. He turned to Gardner Fox, who wrote many JSA stories, to craft a new team with artist Mike Sekowsky in the anthology title *The Brave and the Bold*. Extraterrestrial refugee Martian Manhunter joined Flash and Green Lantern, newly reimagined from their 1940s iterations, as did Wonder Woman, Aquaman, Superman and Batman—plus that teenage sidekick Snapper Carr. The regular series began later that year, with Superman's and Batman's roles shrinking in favor of early arrivals Green Arrow and the Atom.

The title immediately became one of DC's Top 10 sellers in 1961, surpassing the Flash's and Green Lantern's solo series. (It also inspired Stan Lee and Jack Kirby to create a team book, *The Fantastic Four*.)

Read on for a full historical look back at the League—in all its incarnations.

1960
FIRST APPEARANCE

The original seven heroes— Aquaman, Batman, Flash, Green Lantern, Martian Manhunter, Superman and Wonder Woman—battle Starro the Conqueror, a giant alien starfish bent on world domination in the League's debut story in *The Brave and the Bold* #28. Snapper Carr joins as the team's nonpowered, finger-snapping, hipster mascot.

REGULAR SERIES BEGINS

Justice League of America launches its long-running regular series with a classic cover pitting the Flash against the dimension-hopping tyrant Despero.

1961

1962

"AS EACH METEOR LANDED, ITS OCCUPANT WOULD BREAK ITS SHELL AND EMERGE IN ITS TRUE FORM! THEN WITH ITS SPECIAL POWERS IT WOULD TURN THE INHABITANTS OF EARTH TO LIFE— FORMS SIMILAR TO ITS OWN.."

"COMMANDING THE ARMY OF THESE TRANSMUTED CREATURES, EACH WOULD WAGE ALL-OUT WAR WITH ONE ANOTHER UNTIL ONLY ONE REMAINED..."

1962

1963

1961
GREEN ARROW JOINS

Just four issues in, the League gets its first new member as Oliver Queen's alter ego signs up for duty. The archer's presence changes the complexion of the team; two issues later Batman and Superman are listed for the first time as "non-participating members" in the roll call.

1962
A BELATED ORIGIN STORY

The JLA's origin story is finally told in flashback. Seven aliens from distant Appellax arrive on Earth intending to battle one another. The League forms to drive them off.

A SMALL WONDER

Billed as "the world's smallest superhero," the Atom proves his worthiness to join after saving the League from, yes, a booby-trapped bowling ball.

1963
WORLDS COLLIDE

With previous comics establishing that the Justice Society of America (the 1940s prototype for the JLA) still existed on "Earth-Two," the two teams met in the first of a series of annual crossovers. The League also encounters Black Canary, who eventually crosses worlds to join the Justice League.

1964
TAKING A FLIER

The extraterrestrial contingent of the League grows with the induction of Hawkman, a winged visitor from planet Thanagar. (Hawkgirl, meanwhile, is lamely told that only one new member is allowed at a time.)

A (Brief) History of the Justice League

1969
NO MORE TEEN SIDEKICKS

Once included to give kids someone to identify with, non-powered teenage mascots soon grew passé. In the last *Justice League* issue of the 1960s, the Joker tricks Snapper Carr into betraying the team, which he subsequently quits.

1970
INTO SPACE

The first issue of the 1970s saw a major scenery change, as the JLA decamped from its Secret Sanctuary to an enormous satellite headquarters in Earth's orbit.

1973
TEEN SIDEKICKS RETURN . . . ON TV

ABC airs the first *Super Friends* cartoon episode featuring the original core Justice League, minus Martian Manhunter, Flash and Green Lantern. Robin is included, as are sidekicks created for the show, Wendy, Marvin and Wonder Dog. Later seasons included TV creations Wonder Twins Zan and Jayna and their monkey Gleek—as well as comics characters Firestorm and Cyborg.

1975
NAME TAGS WOULD'VE HELPED

After a mind-scrambler leads to the heroes going home to the wrong secret identities, the League members share their real names with one another.

1973

1979

1987

1979

1992

1979
THE EVIL LEAGUE

The League—now including android Red Tornado—temporarily falls prey to a body-switching scheme with the Secret Society of Super-Villains.

1985
CRISIS STRIKES

A much-changed League featuring Elongated Man, Vixen, Steel, Gypsy, Vibe and Zatanna Zatara confronts the "Crisis on Infinite Earths," the massive crossover event that winnowed the multiple Earths into a single streamlined universe. The JLA's satellite is destroyed in the process.

1987
NEW TEAM

A new series relaunches the team, now including Guy Gardner, an abrasive Green Lantern. The title for several years becomes Justice League International, reflecting the team's global responsibilities.

1992
DEATH OF SUPERMAN

The Justice League battles the alien monstrosity Doomsday alongside Superman, who is killed in one of the best-selling comics of all time. The sequence would later serve as a foundation for events depicted in *Batman v Superman: Dawn of Justice.*

1997

1996
KINGDOM COME

Mark Waid and Alex Ross's seminal miniseries imagines a future in which too many superheroes and supervillains become a calamity for Earth, forcing the JLA to reassemble and tame the metahuman masses.

1997
NEW WORLD ORDER

The original high-powered hero lineup reunites against a new enemy: the White Martians. The Grant Morrison story line led off JLA, a revival that ran for 126 issues and nine years.

2001
BACK TO TELEVISION

Nine years after *Batman: The Animated Series* introduced a noir look to DC universe cartoons, the team gets the same treatment in Justice League. Adding Hawkgirl and John Stewart's Green Lantern to the core lineup, the series ran two seasons with three more as *Justice League Unlimited*.

2003
UNIVERSES COLLIDE!

While a JLA crossover with Marvel's Avengers had been teased since the 1980s, the two publishers finally came to terms in 2003 with JLA/Avengers—or Avengers/JLA, depending on which publisher printed the issue you were reading.

2004

2006

1992

2016

2004
IDENTITY CRISIS

Mystery novelist Brad Meltzer's acclaimed *Identity Crisis* miniseries uses the murder of the Elongated Man's wife, Sue Dibny, to take the heroes to task for the forcible altering of others' memories, a frequent trope in early stories to protect secret identities. The truth behind her death nearly tears the team apart.

2006
WONDER WOMAN RESTORED

The 2006 relaunch of the *Justice League of America* series undid the postcrisis deletion of Wonder Woman from the League's origins, brought in a new JLA Satellite and further made Batman, Superman and Wonder Woman central to the decision to form a permanent team.

2011
THE NEW 52

Yet another relaunch pits Batman, Green Lantern, Superman and Cyborg against minions of Darkseid, setting up elements for the later films.

2016
REBIRTH

The most recent relaunch, the Rebirth-era League has the same basic members as the cinematic cast, plus two Green Lanterns. Because just one isn't enough.

BATMAN

In His Own League

GOTHAM'S
BROODING
VIGILANTE DOESN'T
EXACTLY PLAY WELL
WITH OTHERS. BUT
BY UNITING
FORMIDABLE GODS
AND UPSTART
HEROES, THE DARK
KNIGHT FINDS
HIMSELF AT THE
CENTER OF AN ALL-
POWERFUL TEAM.

By Sean Howe

◄

Concept art for
Ben Affleck's
Batman in
Justice League.

BATMAN IS A LONER TO THE CORE—ALWAYS has been. One need look no further than his origin story, at the indelible solitary images that have marked every telling of his tale since 1939: alone and kneeling over his murdered parents, alone and lifting weights, alone in his study when a single bat flies by. As played by Ben Affleck in *Batman v Superman: Dawn of Justice,* he's also angry. At the outset of 2016's heavyweight matchup between comic-book titans, the brooding Dark Knight had been engaged in vigilante vengeance for 20 years before Superman comes along and threatens his monopoly on the costumed crime-fighting racket.

Maybe it was a pang of impotence that ate at Bruce Wayne when Superman arrived in Metropolis and diminished him to navigating city streets in a Jeep Renegade and staring up at burning buildings. Maybe it was simple jealousy, stoked by the worshipful headlines that praised Superman's heroics: Batman never stopped missiles or saved a school bus. Who was this powerful immigrant stepping on his turf, and what were the limits of his power? When Batman finally did meet Superman, he had only one question: "Do you bleed?"

How did we get to this point? Historically the Batman of the comics has been far more cordial to his fellow superheroes. After all, it was his idea, at the dawn of the 1960s, to found the Justice League, a suggestion that came in *Justice League of America #9*. Batman, safely in his Bat-Plane, drops a hook to drag away some Kryptonite so that Superman can defeat a creature made of diamond. "We ought to form a club or society," Batman suggests after landing. It seemed that Bruce Wayne craved companionship after all.

But that didn't mean all was always harmonious. Within the Justice League, Batman was set apart by being the only one among the founders without powers. And so it happened that in the first issues of the group's own comic, Batman watched Superman from the sidelines, provided lifts to stranded bystanders, and was left behind with teenage hipster and team mascot Snapper Carr—as bait. It's enough to make anyone a little testy.

Despite the demands of Gotham City, Batman maintained a good attendance record with the League, and he could be reliably spotted in the background at meetings, quietly sitting at the conference table. But once in a while bitterness boiled to the surface. "How about me?!" he asks Superman when a pack of villains attacks everyone else. "It bugs me that they didn't even think enough of Batman to try and stop him! Man, that hurts!"

As the 1960s wore on, the *Batman* television show—featuring a teen sidekick, Robin—ensured that the world at large saw the Dark Knight as just another camp sensation, with no regard for his painful past. But by the early 1970s it was

> ❝ He's got to overcome his misanthropic tendencies. He's kind of a loner. He has to get past that ❞
>
> —*Ben Affleck*

backpedaling time, and Batman regained his frown and recovered some of his early antisocial behavior.

When he participated in Justice League shenanigans, the World's Greatest Detective still lurked in the background, flipping switches or reading printouts. But now he was prideful, even aloof. Batman shone brightest when someone was needed to cast doubt on a plan or point a finger in someone's ribs.

Throughout the 1980s, tensions with Superman increased, and it became clear that the Kryptonian's adherence to rules was getting under Batman's antiauthoritarian skin. He quit the Justice League over the group's refusal to intercede in a sovereign country's civil war without permission from the U.S. State Department.

▲
Top: *Justice League of America* #9, picturing Batman's assist of Superman prior to suggesting a team-up. Bottom: Snapper Carr from 1961's *JLA* #3—the team's only other nonpowered member.

▶
Justice League Batman concept art.

Batman

In Frank Miller's *The Dark Knight Returns,* an older version of the character saw Superman as a weapon of a hawkish government and resolved to destroy him.

Although that story took place in an alternate DC Universe, it became arguably the most influential of all Batman comics; its violent rage shoots through *Batman v Superman,* and parts of Miller's text—like Bruce Wayne leading an underground army—are even glimpsed in that film's dream sequences.

After a stint stalking around in the Justice League International, in which he famously knocked out a loudmouth member with a single punch, Batman retired from group activity. In the wake of *The Dark Knight Returns* and the blockbuster 1989 *Batman* movie, his most popular quality seemed to be his grim demeanor.

DC has lately reset its universes and rebooted its characters at a head-spinning pace, and through multiple dimensions and realities, Batman's services are usually required at whichever incarnation of the JLA is around. He's still got his flair for stubborn individuality. When a group of unfriendly White Martians attacks, it's Batman's very humanity that provides him with cover—without superpowers, he's below the radar of the invading aliens.

When perennial Batman foe Ra's al Ghul decides that the best shot for the animal kingdom is fewer humans and begins taking down the Justice League one by one, it turns out that the reconnaissance came from Batman himself. The moody hero had been keeping files on the weaknesses of his teammates in case of an emergency. They feel betrayed, but really, how could they be surprised that the distrustful lone wolf in their midst would keep contingency plans?

By the end of *Batman v Superman,* Batman is facing the prospect of losing his edge to a new generation of heroes coming up from behind—heroes with actual superpowers and more potential. He seizes upon a philosophy: If you can't beat 'em, join 'em, and make yourself useful as a tactical leader.

The night Bruce Wayne's parents were murdered, *Excalibur* was playing at the theater. Perhaps he saw himself in the Arthurian tradition when he wielded a sword against Superman; now, he realizes, it's time for the Dark Knight to form his own Round Table. As he stood over Clark Kent's grave, he turned to Wonder Woman with a plea: "Help me find the others like you." By co-opting a piece of the future, this Batman is securing a place at the head of the table. If he's a father figure to the new generation, he can shape them to fulfill his own goals.

"What are your superpowers again?" the Flash asks Batman in *Justice League.* The reply: "I'm rich." This is the Batman for our times, pulling strings with his inheritance, surrounded by powerful colleagues but ultimately, inevitably...alone.

▲
Top: Ben Affleck took on the role of Bruce Wayne for the first time in 2016's *Batman v Superman: Dawn of Justice.* Bottom: As Batman, he faced off against Henry Cavill's Superman.

▶
2000's *JLA: Tower of Babel* story line revealed Batman kept secret records on each of his colleagues, extensively detailing the best ways to take them down. (If necessary, of course.)

DRIVING LESSONS

Batman wouldn't be Batman without a fleet of vehicles for every purpose—all painted in his trademark black, of course. Here's what you need to know about what's new. **BY NICOLE SPERLING**

THE KNIGHTCRAWLER

Part giant motorcycle, part tank and part steel crab: It's the perfect vehicle to get Batman through those hard-to-maneuver locales. "I loved the idea that when you first see it, it's sitting low, its legs are folded up, it's traveling flat, and it looks like a tank," says production designer Patrick Tatopoulos. "And then suddenly it stands up on its legs, and you can see the proportions of the thing. It's enormous, and it can actually climb up walls. The audience is going to love it."

THE FLYING FOX

A legacy vehicle originally created by Bruce Wayne's father, the Flying Fox is what happens when you meld a fighter jet with a cargo airplane. Bruce upgrades his father's design so the massive vehicle can transport his league of superheroes (along with all his vehicles). "When you put the two together, it looks like the Flying Fox had a baby, and the baby is the Batmobile," Tatopoulos says. Three stories tall, the Flying Fox is his favorite creation. "I think you can build a character out of a jet, and I think the Flying Fox has become a real character in the film," he says.

THE BATMOBILE

When Tatopoulos began constructing worlds for *Batman v Superman: Dawn of Justice*, he homed in on the Batmobile to help define his hero's aesthetic. Here the Batmobile is upgraded to reflect its driver's tough and rugged exterior. "It's now more of an off-road vehicle," Tatopoulos says. "Instead of a jeep you drive in the city, you take this one on a Desert Storm mission. It's still elegant, but it's part of a language that includes trucks and tanks and power."

Amazon Prime

WONDER WOMAN LIT UP THE SUMMER BOX OFFICE WITH HER WISDOM AND POSITIVITY— NOT TO MENTION HER BADASS BATTLEFIELD MOVES. NEXT UP? SHE'S POISED TO BECOME THE JUSTICE LEAGUE'S MVP.

By Caleb Goellner

◄
Gal Gadot's
Justice League
Wonder Woman
costume.

"IS SHE WITH YOU?"

An incredulous Superman looked on in disbelief as Diana, Princess of Themyscira, showed up unannounced at the conclusion of *Batman v Superman: Dawn of Justice* with her best warrior face on as the two heroes were at their worst. After waging war on one another, they faced certain death at the hands of Doomsday. Just like that, Wonder Woman saved them not only from a world-ending threat but also from their baser natures. And that battlefield show-down was well before Gal Gadot dominated the box office this past summer, starring in her own epic origin story—a film that stands as the year's second-highest-grossing film and one of the most acclaimed superhero movies of all time.

In the space of just two films Wonder

Woman destroyed the literal personification of war and made sworn enemies see the best in each other. The message? Bad guys had better watch out.

From her inception, Wonder Woman was designed as a force for goodness—a heroine who would fight to protect all that is right. William Moulton Marston and artist Harry G. Peter ushered her into the world in 1941, telling her origin in *All-Star Comics* #8. The series starred the super-team precursor to the Justice League known as the Justice Society of America, and it was a big deal. Superhero comics as we know them today were still in their relative youth, and very few costumed women were fighting crime when Diana debuted, let alone fighting Nazis.

Marston combined this marketplace observation with personal inspiration. A psychologist and the developer of an early lie-detection technique, he believed that women should run the world. His convictions weren't necessarily a template for present day wokeness, but they were revolutionary in his day, particularly in comics. Wonder Woman throwing off the shackles of her oppressors was akin to her breaking the chains of patriarchy.

His wife, fellow psychologist Elizabeth Holloway Marston, and his lover Olive Byrne were noted inspirations for his idealized superhero. The story goes that Holloway Marston helped her husband create a female superhero, while bracelets worn by Byrne factored into Wonder Woman's costume design. It's safe to assume Holloway Marston was no small influence on Wonder Woman's Lasso of Truth, to boot, as a contributor to the lie-detection work credited to her husband. Diana Prince's unfailing strength represented Marston's belief that women were actually stronger in most respects than men.

Wonder Woman's origin initially went something like this: Queen Hippolyta of the Amazons, desperate for a child, sculpted a daughter from clay. Moved, Aphrodite, the goddess of love, brought her to life. Thus Princess Diana was born. She trained in the ways of her people, earned some cool gear and set off to the

> **"She loves humankind, she loves all people—but she doesn't feel as much a part of them as she would like"**
> —*Gal Gadot*

world of men after injured American soldier Steve Trevor crashed up on her shores. She was ready to show a warring world a better way. She wasn't out for revenge; she wasn't a lonely survivor of a dead planet; she was simply good.

And she was a huge hit. Wonder Woman's earliest stories cast her as a fish out of water navigating a new world with curiosity and empathy. Living by her Amazonian values, she met each conflict with decisive action, even if she'd usually turn to her mother for a moralizing sum-up at the end of an adventure.

Readers got more Diana a month later in *Sensation Comics* #1, and by the time *Wonder Woman* #1 dropped in 1942, the character's core elements were in place: tiara-topped red-white-and-blue costume,

▲
Wonder Woman landed her first cover in January 1942 and spun off into her own series by July of that same year (left). *Wonder Woman* #1 shared Diana Prince's origin: molded from clay by Hippolyte (later Hippolyta) and brought to life by Aphrodite. Right: by the early 1960s Wonder Woman's look evolved to include hot pants in *Justice League* #9.

►
Wonder Woman concept art.

Lasso of Truth, bulletproof bracelets. Still, despite the empowering ideals of her creators, Wonder Woman found herself cast in more mundane roles almost immediately. After her first team-up with the Justice Society of America in 1942, Wonder Woman was thrilled to accept an offer to be the team's …secretary. Twenty years on, however, times had begun to change. In 1962's *Justice League of America #9*, Wonder Woman helps tell the team's origin story as a cofounder, a mere receptionist no more.

Diana Prince would occasionally find herself stuck behind a desk in the 1970s television series starring Lynda Carter— though most often the secretary getup was as part of a secret identity. Over three seasons Carter's upbeat, peace-loving Wonder Woman would help win WWII, bust crime rings, thwart alien invasions and skateboard like a champ. Carter's sunny take on the character helped to define the heroine for a generation of fans.

As for comics, the mid-'80s up through 2010 ushered in a warrior-diplomat era for the character. Following DC's line-rebooting Crisis on Infinite Earths event, *Wonder Woman #1* launched to establish the hero as the linchpin in a new Greek mythology. By 2003 Wonder Woman headed a Themysciran embassy in America and got involved in geopolitical conflicts. In her roles as a seasoned hero, businesswoman and politician, Diana inspired everyone around her.

Relaunched with a new #1 issue in 2011 and again in 2016, Wonder Woman's ongoing title became focused on fine-tuning her origin even further. Now she was the daughter of Queen Hippolyta and Zeus, and her divine ancestry set her on a course to oppose Ares and ultimately defeat the God of War in Patty Jenkins's stand-alone film, a soaring saga that embraced blue skies, optimism and warm, subtle humor without falling prey to overt sentiment.

Seven and a half decades on, she's still making history. She's more than a symbol who resonates across generations; she's an enduring powerhouse. Matched against the boys, she's the equal of Superman when they have engaged, usually battling the Man of Steel to a draw. When sheer might isn't enough, she's every bit the tactician as Batman. There's hardly a DC hero she hasn't bested.

Now a much-needed presence on the Justice League, Gadot's Diana is flanked by heroes who could stand to learn some lessons from the powerful Amazon. She is wise, radiating hope in a world corrupted by fear, and her strength derives from her purity of spirit, her innate goodness, her dogged persistence. Couple that with unparalleled battle skills and unfailing instincts? Wonder Woman surely stands to be the team's greatest asset.

"Is she with you?" Superman asked. No, Supes, we're all with her.

Additional reporting by Anthony Breznican

▲
Gal Gadot made her first feature-length appearance as Wonder Woman in director Patty Jenkins's epic adventure this past summer (though the character is only ever referred to her onscreen by her given name, Diana).

▶
A 2016 variant cover of *Wonder Woman #7*.

SPECIAL FORCES

The Amazons of Themyscira have a role to play in *Justice League*—even if Wonder Woman remains offshore.
BY NICOLE SPERLING

WELCOME TO THE *OTHER* SIDE OF THE ISLE. The water runs crystal clear and the Amazons who reside there are still glorious warriors, but unlike the sunny, idyllic locale we visited in *Wonder Woman*, over on this side the Amazons are charged with guarding an important artifact left on Themyscira by the aliens of Apokolips. "We Amazons were here when the aliens first arrived," says Danish actress Connie Nielsen, who reprises her role as Queen Hippolyta in the new film. "And we are the ones who make sure these boxes [that belong to the Apokoliptian aliens] would never leave again."

When creating the design for this never-before-glimpsed portion of the magical island, production designer Patrick Tatopoulos wanted to give it a similar feel to the cities portrayed in *Wonder Woman* but differentiate it enough to convey the Amazons' lengthy history on Themyscira.

"Our architecture feels a little bit like Mycenaean architecture: big, gigantic stones, less refined than what you would find on *Wonder Woman*'s Themyscira," Tatopoulos says. "It's like when you go to Greece and you see the Parthenon on the top of Acropolis and it's got the elegant, super-worked-out lines and proportions. Then you go back to Mycenae, Greece, to an earlier temple, and you have some bold, simple gigantic stones—more primitive architecture. It still has curves, but we are going further back in time when we tell this story."

So far back, it should be said, that Hippolyta sports a crown with a cavelike feel

that Nielsen says you have to see to believe (those Amazons know a thing or two about impressive headwear). The period in question is also long before Diana's birth, dating to when the Amazons first encountered the alien visitors. "You get to see thousands of years of Amazons," Nielsen says.

Between uniting heroes and fighting off world-ending threats, Diana doesn't spend much time at her childhood home in *Justice League*. But make no mistake—her fearsome female tribe will be every bit as impressive as they were in the summer's box office smash starring Gal Gadot and Nielsen, whose warrior prowess will be on display once more. "You see them do battle—it's an incredible battle," Nielsen says. Spoken like a true queen.

▲
Above left: Concept art for the ancient building on Themyscira. Right: The Amazons guard the artifact.

◄
Concept art for Hippolyta.

In His Element

JASON MOMOA BRINGS SMOLDER AND SWAGGER TO HIS UNDERWATER SUPERHERO. PREPARE TO MEET THE NEW AQUAMAN.

By Oliver Sava

◄

Justice League concept art for Jason Momoa's rugged Aquaman.

RAW INTENSITY. BADASS ATTITUDE. UNDENI- able sex appeal. Not the first three qualities you'd think of when it comes to a superhero who can talk to fish. But thanks to Jason Momoa, the actor who embodied warrior fury and passion as Dothraki leader Khal Drogo on HBO juggernaut *Game of Thrones*, Aquaman is getting a full-on bad-boy makeover—chugging bourbon in the rain, standing stoically before huge crashing waves, riding ene-mies like surfboards into battle. Pardon us while we swoon.

It's a pretty radical departure from the blond-haired, blue-eyed white-bread Aquaman popularized by the long-running *Super Friends* cartoons. *Super Friends* might have made Aquaman a household name, but it also turned him into a pop-culture punch line (*Entourage*, anyone?) because he wasn't as cool as his big-name teammates Batman, Superman and Wonder Woman—admittedly a tall bar but one Momoa seems likely to leap with ease.

Arthur "Aquaman" Curry debuted in 1941's *More Fun Comics #73*, appearing in a backup story by DC editor Mort Weisinger and artist Paul Norris. One of three major characters created by Weisinger that year—Johnny Quick and Green Arrow being the other two—Aquaman was originally the son of a famous undersea explorer who raised his child in a watertight palace in the ancient ruins of Atlantis. In his first appearance, Aquaman comes to the rescue of refugees after their ship is attacked by a Nazi submarine, and it made a lot of sense to have a water-based hero when there was a world war being fought at sea.

Even though his first story has him punching out Nazis, Aquaman isn't remembered as a wartime hero. The character's popularity grew when creators started exploring the aquatic world around Arthur Curry. His origin story was changed so that he gained his power from his mother's Atlantean heritage, and as the city of Atlantis developed, Aquaman gained a new supporting cast: Aqualad the sidekick, Mera the love interest (see sidebar), Nuidis Vulko the adviser. Arthur's half brother Orm became the villainous Ocean Master, and he would often face off against the mercenary Black Manta, who delivered one of the greatest blows to the hero when he murdered Arthur and Mera's toddler son.

Aquaman has been a member of the Justice League of America since its first appearance in 1960's *The Brave and the Bold #28*, but his big shot at leading his own incarnation of the Justice League is widely considered a low point. The Justice League Detroit era has its charms, but it failed to grab readers with its lineup of newer heroes that lacked the popularity of DC's heavy hitters. Only when both Aquaman himself and the team dramatically changed would he become a regular fixture once more.

In 1997 *JLA #1* brought all of DC's

> **"Aquaman is misunderstood. He's a loner who doesn't play by the rules. Zack Snyder really wanted [him to be like] the outlaw Josey Wales"**
>
> —*Jason Momoa*

biggest names together, and this new direction reinvigorated the team while showing how a more aggressive Aquaman worked within a group. Nearly every superhero received an extreme, gritty makeover in the '90s—Aquaman was no exception. He grew long hair and a beard, and in an especially shocking twist, he lost his left hand when it was fed to piranhas. This gave the character a grizzled new attitude and a costume change that saw his hand replaced with a harpoon. He also lost his orange shirt and started wearing a piece of armor that covered his right shoulder and arm, a look echoed in Momoa's costume for *Justice League*.

The new film is heavily inspired by the *Justice League* comic that debuted as part of DC Comics' New 52 relaunch in 2011, an

▲
Top left: Aquaman faces off against Nazis in his initial 1941 run. Top right: the Ocean Master, a classic villain from 1966's *Aquaman #29*.

▶
Right: concept art for Momoa's Aquaman. Below: the version popularized by the cartoon *Super Friends* starting in 1973.

initiative that also attempted to make Aquaman a bigger presence in the DC Universe. Geoff Johns, current president and chief creative officer of DC Entertainment, was the writer of both *Justice League* and *Aquaman* at the time, and the two series crossed over with a story that put Aquaman in the middle of a war between Atlantis and the surface world.

That connection to DC's flagship title boosted Arthur's profile for a short while, but once Johns left *Aquaman,* the character began to drift from prominence again. The *Aquaman* series has been beholden to Johns's vision for the past few years, but that changed this summer as writer Dan Abnett and artist Stjepan Sejić turned the comic book into a smoldering underwater urban fantasy.

Aquaman is sexiest when he's more rugged, and the current *Aquaman* comic is embracing this philosophy, echoing what Momoa is serving up onscreen. (Sejić has a background in both atmospheric superhero dramas and erotic romantic comedies, and he's a smart addition to the creative team at a time when Aquaman's movie persona is so heavily defined by sex appeal.) Sejić brings a sultry quality to the character with the return of Arthur Curry's beard and long hair, and the entire book is made more attractive by Sejić's digital painting, which does beautiful things with color and light as it explores a lush underwater environment.

The marine world offers a plethora of visual opportunities, and while the majesty of this setting has been explored in animation—most significantly in Disney's *The Little Mermaid* and Pixar's *Finding Nemo* franchise—live-action movies typically go underwater for darker stories that lean toward horror. Momoa's stand-alone *Aquaman* film hits the big screen in 2018 and will be directed by James Wan, who became known in the industry with such horror movies as *Saw, The Conjuring* and *Insidious.* His crash course in explosive action—2015's *Fast 7*—suggests that he'll merge underwater chills with superhero thrills.

The success of Disney's *Moana* proved

that there's an audience hungry for Pacific Islander representation—that film greatly benefited from the inspiration it pulled from real-world tribes with a strong connection to the water. Similarly, casting a Hawaiian actor and outfitting him with tribal tattoos (ones that echo the actor's own, in a moment of onscreen synergy) indicates that Warner Bros. is shifting Aquaman into a new cultural milieu, and while it's too early to tell how that might alter Arthur Curry's story, it's a promising change. Momoa's casting makes the Justice League a more inclusive team at the same time it completely redefines Aquaman as a hard-hitting, hard-living hero.

At long last, Arthur Curry has become a real force of nature.

▲
Top right: artwork from Stjepan Sejić's 2017 *Aquaman* #25. Top left and below: In stark contrast are the 1960 and 1961 comics *The Brave and the Bold* #28 and Aquaman and Aqualad's *Showcase Comics* #31, portraying Aquaman as a blond-haired denizen of the sea.

UNDER THE SEA

Costume designer Michael Wilkinson brings Aquaman's rugged bad-boy look to life with elaborate tattoos, gold armor and a few special-effects tricks. **BY NICOLE SPERLING**

★ **Given Aquaman's intricate** tattoos, hulking frame and intense gaze, it's no wonder Jason Momoa's superhero was costume designer Michael Wilkinson's favorite character to imagine. "Creating a costume for Jason and his amazing superhero physique was fantastic," he gushes. Wilkinson drew inspiration from the tribal tattoos that dominate the actor's sizable chest for Arthur Curry's underwater armor, using computer technology to perfect the scales that adorn the costume. "The scales were done in a way that would have been impossible to sculpt by hand because they are so incredibly detailed and perfectly repeated around his body," Wilkinson says. "They are almost like the 3D extrapolation of his tattoos." Sharp-eyed fans may notice that the left bracer mimics the triangular shark-teeth motif of Momoa's very real tattoo on his forearm.

But the armor alone wasn't enough to sell the full aquatic effect. Since Momoa's underwater scenes were shot on a large, dry soundstage—all the water was added in postproduction—the crew doused Mamoa's garb with an oily overlay to make the costume look wet and to add a cool, sleek factor. Says Wilkinson: "There was a final wet-down before each scene to make sure [the costumes] were glossy and beautiful."

THE LIFE AQUATIC

Justice League will offer audiences an important first glimpse of the kingdom of Atlantis, home to troubled hero Arthur Curry, known to the world as Aquaman. **BY NICOLE SPERLING**

LIFE IS ROUGH AT THE BOTTOM OF THE SEA. At least it is for Arthur Curry, the superhero who believes his own people killed his mother, Queen Atlanna. When he encounters the heroes of the Justice League, he's grappling with grief and anger and trying to find a place of his own. Says actor Jason Momoa: "He's misunderstood." He's also in the midst of rescuing a fisherman caught in a big storm—and in the process, he comes across a greater villain than the punishing seas. But this Aquaman isn't one to back away from a conflict. "He's a brawler, and he jumps into the fight—gaining a little more knowledge about what the stakes are," Momoa adds.

While the specific circumstances of Arthur's personal story will be the subject of 2018's stand-alone Aquaman film—which also stars Nicole Kidman as the ill-fated Atlanna, Amber Heard as Arthur's bride, Mera, and Willem Dafoe as key ally Nuidis Vulko—*Justice League* will serve as a valuable introduction to the aquatic character and his unusual home.

According to production designer Patrick Tatopoulos, the ocean kingdom is a representation of the traveling culture of the Atlanteans. The Atlantis glimpsed in *Justice League* will be a far more expansive version of the underwater civilization than some earlier iterations. "This ancient city looks like an aesthetically pleasing postapocalyptic world," Tatopoulos says. "[The Atlanteans] have seen South America. They have seen Greece. They have

seen North Africa. When you pull all this together, it doesn't matter where the island was, it's an island that mixes multiple looks and cultures." The design for the tattoos and trinkets that adorn Momoa's body are rooted in that cultural melange.

When it comes to underwater action, however, the actor says that whatever he might have had to endure during the *Justice League* shoot, it was a lazy swim in the sea compared with his solo outing—he often had to wear 40 extra pounds of armor strapped to his back as part of his regal Atlantean costume. "What ended up hurting is adding 40 pounds to your fight scene," Momoa says. "Forty additional pounds . . . throws everything out of whack." Here's betting this Aquaman can still land a punch with the best of 'em.

▲
Concept art of Atlantis. All underwater scenes were shot on a stage, with water added digitally in postproduction.

★ **Ruling the Ocean Kingdom** with her dear husband, Aquaman, Mera, the Queen of Atlantis, is a warrior and a sorceress who is able to manipulate water with her mind. We're given only a glimpse of the regal figure played by actress Amber Heard in *Justice League*—she'll get way more screen time in *Aquaman,* out Dec. 21, 2018—but if her getup for this fall's massive superhero mash-up is any indication, her powers will be vast. According to costume designer Michael Wilkinson (*Batman v Superman: Dawn of Justice*), the goal was to create for Mera an armored suit built specifically for the waves. "Her costume is made out of a really interesting material," he says. "It's see-through, so when the light hits her, it has a beautiful effect, almost like a fish scale. You can see light through it, which gives it a supernatural quality." Consider us bewitched.

Full Speed Ahead

EZRA MILLER'S HIGH-SPIRITED QUIPPY YOUNGSTER BRINGS SOME HIPSTER COOL TO THE STATELY LEAGUE OF HEROES.
By Noel Murray

◄

Concept art of Ezra Miller's costumed take on the Flash for *Justice League.*

LEAVE IT TO THE FLASH TO BE IN TWO PLACES at the same time.

When *Justice League* arrives in theaters in November, speedy, crimson-clad Barry Allen, played by actor Ezra Miller (*Fantastic Beasts and Where to Find Them*), will be among the intimidating clan of superfriends. Fresh out of his teens, Barry is like a geeky, overeager kid enjoying what he can do, giddy with the spirit of possibility—just imagine if you could dodge nearly any danger and wrap up nearly any crisis in record time? He knows he's a relative rookie, and he's excited to stand alongside his more experienced counterparts. "Barry's in total awe of them," Miller told *EW* earlier this year. As for Ezra himself? "I was definitely feeling like Barry, stepping into the big leagues."

Of course, right around the same time Miller will be racing into multiplexes, Grant Gustin will be zipping around Central City on the CW's hit series *The Flash*—as he's done since the show debuted in 2014. That means fans of the Scarlet Speedster will have the rare opportunity to watch the adventures of one superfast character named Barry Allen in a movie theater and then go home to watch an entirely different Barry dash around on TV.

In a weird way, though, having two separate Flashes in two different places is true to the whole history of the character. In nearly every incarnation, the Flash—especially the one with Barry Allen behind the mask—has been the DC Comics hero most likely to travel between dimensions and fight bad guys who look a lot like himself. That's also been the key to his longevity and popularity. After Superman, Batman and Wonder Woman, the Flash has been DC's most enduring character, beloved from generation to generation. His appeal is simple: He can lead a hundred lives in the time it takes most of us to get through one.

While he looks like a youth, the character actually debuted in 1956 in *Showcase #4*. The issue took an original Golden Age version of the Flash named Jay Garrick from the '40s and reimagined him as Barry Allen: a police scientist who gains superspeed after he's doused with lightning-enhanced chemicals. He was a hero designed for the accelerated pace of the Atomic Age, and artist Carmine Infantino and writer Robert Kanigher were largely responsible for his creation.

The Barry Allen Flash was a new kind of champion for a new kind of comic, which could be unapologetically silly, impressively nerdy and nearly always infused with Kennedy-era optimism. In 1961's *The Flash #123* "Flash of Two Worlds!" written by Gardner Fox and drawn by Infantino, the story sees the speedy superhero moving so quickly that he slips from his own universe to a parallel one—later dubbed Earth-Two—where he meets the Jay Garrick Flash.

> " I was definitely nervous and excited every single day...stepping into the big leagues with this incredible group of collaborators "
>
> —*Ezra Miller*

With that one whimsical story, Fox and Infantino changed the comic scene. Their introduction of the concept of the "multiverse," with different versions of the same DC heroes strewn across countless versions of Earths, was revolutionary. Since that comic, the Flash has visited—or faced enemies from—many other Earths.

The Flash long retained his sense of whimsy, but when superhero stories took a dark turn in the 1980s, even the upbeat character found himself a little short on happy endings. In a story line that threaded from the death of Barry's wife, Iris, in *The Flash #275* to the end of the original run of the title in *The Flash #350*, the character stood trial for killing his archenemy Reverse-Flash. The arc ended with Barry fleeing to the far future, where

▲ Above left: *Showcase Comics #4*, an October 1956 issue, introduced Barry Allen as the Flash. Above right: Barry Allen meets his counterpart on another Earth, Jay Garrick, in 1961's *The Flash #123*.

► Ezra Miller (in concept art) describes putting on his costume as "a very long, delicate process, where everyone was afraid of everything breaking. I would feel like a Victorian lady with my chambermaids."

he was reunited with a reincarnated version of Iris, only to be killed off during the DC-universe-altering maxi-series Crisis on Infinite Earths.

Afterward Barry's former sidekick Wally West took up the mantle of the Flash. Under the direction of writer Mark Waid in particular, the Flash mythology evolved into something more like what viewers of the current TV series know, with a multitude of superfast heroes, villains and supernatural entities all drawing on something called the Speed Force.

But fans never lost their affection for Barry Allen. More than 20 years after he died—an eternity in comic-book time—DC brought the character back, only with a much more tragic origin story involving the murder of his mother (Bruce Wayne can relate). Since then, Barry's Flash has been at the center of nearly every major DC Comics event, but his most important recent role has been as the instigator of Flashpoint, an alternate universe formed when Barry went back in time to try to undo his parents' deaths.

Written by DC Comics' president and chief creative officer Geoff Johns, the Flashpoint story line has proved so compelling that it's already served as the basis for an animated movie, a storyline on the CW series and soon will be the title of the character's stand-alone movie, due in 2020. *Batman v Superman: Dawn of Justice* might have teased Flash's role in future films with a scene in which someone who looks like an older Barry Allen in a tattered costume warns Batman of a catastrophe yet to come. That image of the speedster as a voice of doom in a torn-up suit summons up multiple story lines from the comics, including Crisis on Infinite Earths and Flashpoint.

It stands to reason some pretty tough times lie ahead for the movieverse Justice League, and most likely, Allen's about to dash headlong into some potentially world-ending danger. But here's hoping the character hangs on to some of his enthusiasm and youthful spark. His upbeat nature might be just the thing to power him—and his fellow superheroes—through the coming fight.

▲
Clockwise from above left: In 1985 the Flash reset his own comic book timeline, which had been altered by villain Professor Zoom, and reunited with Iris in the 30th Century; the Flash as he appeared in the very first issue of *The Justice League of America* in 1960; and in 1985, the Flash disguised his face when unmasked in court.

▶
Grant Gustin has been starring in the CW's *The Flash* since 2014.

LIGHTNING STRIKE

When creating the design for Flash's crimson outfit, the costume department considered exactly what materials Barry Allen had at hand. **BY NICOLE SPERLING AND DARREN FRANICH**

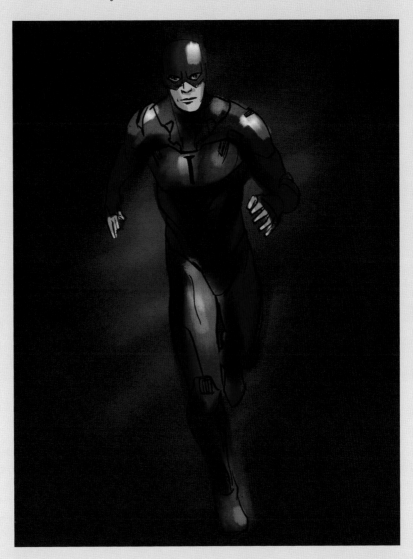

★ **Of course Barry Allen, the** do-it-yourself millennial with super-human speed, would create his own costume. Perhaps he'd use what he had around him. And just maybe he'd break into a super-secret facility to find the latest product advancements that could withstand extreme heat.

At least that was the thinking that went into the Flash's look, a high-performance wicking suit that allows Ezra Miller to move quickly but still feels fashioned at home. Says costume designer Michael Wilkinson: "The suit we see is an interesting combination of being handmade and including ultra-high-tech elements. That's what gives it its personality, high and low tech coming together." It also features an intricate wiring system that turns the Flash into his own energy source. "We have these lines of cir-cuitry criss-crossing his suit that allow him to become an electrical coil," adds Wilkinson. "In the final battle he is able to harness his energy, and you can see it pulsating through the details of his suit."

Fans familiar with the Silver Age iteration of the character might be surprised to learn that Barry won't rely on a certain famous spring-loaded contraption to get into his suit. Says Miller: "I can confirm—spoiler alert—that his suit does not pop out of his ring." Guess this cos-tume has no place for accessories.

TURNING BACK THE CLOCK

Every member of the League has a spinoff in development, but the Flash's solo film might just change the DC movie universe forever.

BY DARREN FRANICH

IN 2011 WRITER GEOFF JOHNS SET THE FLASH on a time-twisting journey that is still reverberating across every conceivable DC universe. In *Flashpoint* Barry Allen awakens in a world that is familiar yet strange. He no longer has superspeed. His dead mother is alive. And the world's heroes are…different. Twisty chronology-resetting chicanery ensues.

Flashpoint altered DC history, setting the stage for a companywide relaunch. So it was a special shock when Warner Bros. announced that *Flashpoint* would be the title of the speedster's solo film. "What fans understand when they hear *Flashpoint*," teases Ezra Miller, "would be almost like hearing a word like 'crisis.' We start to understand that our precious DC universe will inevitably be torn asunder to

an endless, headache-inducing fabric of multiversality. The DC Hyper-Extended Multiverse, as I plan to call it. Quote me!"

He's joking, but the film does have cosmic ramifications. *Flashpoint* has already been adapted twice to the screen, in the animated *Justice League: The Flashpoint Paradox* and on the CW's *The Flash*. But Johns says the live-action film will explore new ground. "There's elements in it that we're going to be playing into that we couldn't do anywhere else," he explains. "The scale of it, the Batman story of it all."

Note: He didn't specify *which* Batman. The Dark Knight of the Flashpoint-verse was Bruce Wayne's father, Thomas, so an older actor might don the cowl. (Heck: Michael Keaton.) But other Justice Leaguers could appear. "In the comics, Cyborg is

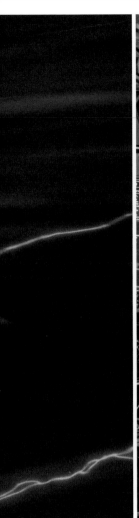

All three images: Ezra Miller in *Justice League*. Putting on the costume was initially a lengthy expedition. "There was a time toward the beginning where it was a very long, delicate process, where everyone was afraid of everything breaking," Miller says with a laugh.

present at Flashpoint in a big way," Ray Fisher reminds us. It's possible that *Flashpoint* could softly reset the continuity of the DC movies, honoring the history people love (hello, Wonder Woman) while eliminating some of the more controversial plot elements (unbreak that neck, Zod!).

But Fisher hasn't seen a script yet—and the film has withstood a few bumps in the road. Warner Bros. first hired Seth Grahame-Smith to direct. When he left, they brought on buzzy *Dope* director Rick Famuyiwa to helm, bringing him onstage at Comic-Con in 2016. But Famuyiwa departed, and the 2018 release date was delayed once more. "The development of the project has been a little Barry Allen-like in its mercurial tendencies," Miller admits. We can't wait.

Heavy Mettle

RAY FISHER'S
CYBORG IS THE
ULTIMATE HYBRID OF
MAN AND MACHINE—
BUT IT'S THE
CHARACTER'S KEEN
INTELLECT AND
BURNING INNER
CONFLICT THAT
HELPED SCORE HIM
AN INVITATION TO
JOIN THE JUSTICE
LEAGUE.
By Noel Murray

◄

Justice League
concept art
for Ray Fisher's
Cyborg.

IN 1980 WRITER MARV WOLFMAN AND ARTIST George Pérez created a handful of new heroes for a revival of the cult-favorite DC Comics title *Teen Titans*. They thought up Raven, the magic-wielding daughter of a world-conquering demon. They came up with Starfire, an alien princess turned slave who escaped to Earth with intergalactic armies on her trail. To bring a little variety to the team, they introduced someone more grounded: a former college athlete named Victor Stone, who'd been severely disfigured in an accident at his parents' cutting-edge laboratory. Vic's scientist father defied his son's wishes, saving his life by fitting him with super-strong robotic body parts. Thus, an ordinary young man was reluctantly reborn as the future superhero Cyborg.

Cyborg arrived in the DC Universe with no dangerous archnemesis for the Titans to defeat, but his everyman personality and nifty electronic gear made him a favorite with fans and with comics creators. After Wolfman and Pérez moved on and the Titans' popularity waned, other writers and artists swooped in to lay claim to the team's best spare part: the kid with all the cybernetics.

Now, after appearing in video games, TV cartoons and DC's animated films, Cyborg, as played by actor Ray Fisher, has finally gotten the biggest upgrade of all: a coveted invitation to join the Justice League before heading his own planned stand-alone film, currently scheduled for early 2020.

When it comes to the history of the character, there's plenty of rich backstory to mine.

As Wolfman and Pérez laid out in the classic one-off issue *Tales of the New Teen Titans* #1 in 1982, Vic Stone grew up caught between two worlds—rebelling against his stuffy academic parents while trying to avoid following friends from his inner-city New York neighborhood down the criminal path.

The accident that transformed his body left him with deep psychological and emotional wounds. He was arguably the strongest of the Titans, with his enhanced arms and legs, robotic eye and seemingly endless supply of gadgets, tools and weapons that he could attach to himself—like a human USB port. But he also had a genius-level intellect and an inferiority complex that left him resentful of both his appearance and the way that so much of his life was forced on him.

Stuck in a comic with DC legacies like Robin, Flash and Wonder Girl, Cyborg was often relegated to a utility role. During the first five years of *New Teen Titans,* his subplots took a backseat to the action surrounding Raven and Starfire. The most famous story arc of the Titans' early years was "The Judas Contract," which involved a turncoat teammate, Tara Markov, and her seduction of Vic's best friend in the group, Gar Logan.

> ❝The fact that he's created of this tech, it puts him in a very unique place. It calls into question himself: Am I just a machine?❞
>
> —*Ray Fisher*

Meanwhile, Cyborg's adventures were much more down-to-earth. He did charity work back in his old neighborhood, helping children with prosthetics to adjust to their new arms and legs. When duty called, he was his team's jack-of-all-trades, providing physical muscle and techno-wizardry. His most memorable story line came late, when he overcame his fear of being more machine than man, thanks to an alien entity named Technis that helped him evolve into a sort of living computer called Cyberion.

In the '90s and early '00s, DC began a cycle of revivals and revamps, trotting out multiple new versions of the Titans and restoring Cyborg to his original self. During the same stretch, Cartoon Network produced an animated version of

▲
Left: Cyborg's first solo cover, the June 1982 *Tales of The New Teen Titans* #1. Right: Victor Stone's tragic backstory revealed in a 1982 issue.

▶
Ray Fisher's Cyborg, revealed briefly in *Batman v Superman,* uses elements from the character's comic-book history.

Cyborg

the Wolfman/Pérez *Teen Titans* (which served as the basis for the much wackier *Teen Titans Go!*), cementing Cyborg as an essential component of a classic team.

Gradually circumstances began to change for Victor Stone, both on and off the page. By the mid-'00s he was becoming more essential to the DCU, included in the crossover adventures alongside the Justice League. In 2006 he appeared a few times on the CW's *Smallville*.

Then in 2011 Cyborg's importance to the DCU became formalized with the company-wide Flashpoint and New 52 events. A massive retrofit turned an alternate-history version of the DC superheroes' origins into canon, and Cyborg was reimagined as someone as essential to protecting the planet as Superman, Batman and Wonder Woman were in other, alternate timelines. In his role as Earth's paramount superhero and resistance leader, Vic Stone even attempts to build his own League.

At his core, though, Vic Stone is a reluctant superhero. Joe Morton, who plays Victor's father, Silas Stone, has said that the upcoming films will dig deeply into Vic's anger with Silas over his dad's treating his body like a piece of machinery, ripe for the tinkering. Judging by the look of the device that jump-starts Cyborg's resurrection in his *Batman v Superman: Dawn of Justice* cameo, the movie version of the character will follow the model of the recent comic-book iteration and will give him a new origin story that involves "fourth-world" alien technology.

More exciting is the fact that *Justice League* and any films that follow can make use of all the character traits that define Vic Stone, from his keen intellect and his resourcefulness to his conflicted feelings over his identity.

Cyborg's secret strength is that his complexity has developed organically, built up by one group of creators after another. Turns out, sometimes classic superheroes are born in moments of wild inspiration. Sometimes they come together piece by piece.

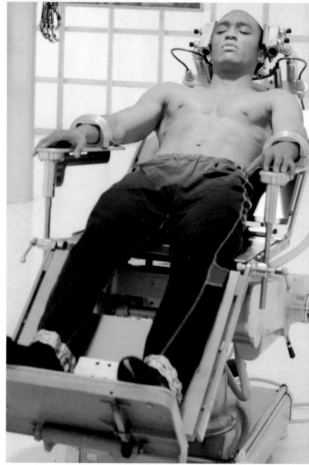

▲
Left: *Teen Titans,* based on George Pérez's comic-book series and featuring Cyborg as a key team member, premiered on Cartoon Network in 2003 and ran five seasons.
Right: The cover of George Pérez and Dick Giordano's *The New Teen Titans Special* from 1980.

▶
The CW's *Smallville* was the first to welcome a live-action Cyborg in 2006. Lee Thompson Young appeared in just three episodes.

TOUGHER THAN STEEL

The football player turned reluctant hero is clad in armor that came from beyond the stars.
BY NICOLE SPERLING

★ **Cyborg is the ultimate modern** superhero: part man, part machine and all configured by the magic of computers.

Costume designer Michael Wilkinson still had a hand in creating his look, though, mostly supplying the CG artists with key elements and texture references for them to rely on. That task was made extra challenging since Cyborg's robotic body is supposedly fashioned by his scientist father out of a material currently not available on planet Earth.

To generate that extraterrestrial feel, Wilkinson's team cast a wide net searching both the natural world and the annals of science fiction for various points of inspiration and reference. "We looked at insects and we looked at robots, liquid metals and reptilian skin," Wilkinson says. "Then we put it all up on a wall and refined what our Cyborg would be."

Although the design team's steady hand was instrumental in differentiating each member of the League, all of the costumes were crafted with an eye toward having the overall ensemble look as compelling as possible onscreen. "It was important to Zack [Synder] that they each have a sense of coming from extremely diverse different worlds," Wilkinson says, "but when you see them together, they look like a team."

WEIRD SCIENCE

In *Justice League,* S.T.A.R. Labs is the domain of Silas Stone—and a gateway to the cosmic science of DC's film universe. **BY DARREN FRANICH**

JOE MORTON KNOWS HIS WAY AROUND groovy futuristic science-fiction sets. In *Terminator 2: Judgment Day,* he was Miles Dyson, chief of killer-robot research at Cyberdyne Systems. Now Morton's playing Dr. Silas Stone, and he admits to feeling a bit of déjà vu when director Zack Snyder showed him Stone's facility. "There was something in my laboratory," Morton recalls, "I think it was a mechanical arm, that really reminded me of *T2.* At one point I think I even joked with Zack, 'So, is this an homage?' He hadn't even realized it!"

If anything, the reverse could be true. First introduced when Skynet was just a mad glimmer in James Cameron's eye, S.T.A.R. Labs has been a key setting in the DC Universe for decades, first appearing in 1971. The name stands for Scientific and Technological Advanced Research Laboratories, and the private company has been the source of various scientific advances. In comics lore, it was the workplace of Silas and his wife, Eleanor, and thus a key location for Cyborg's early *Teen Titans* adventures. Although S.T.A.R. Labs initially referred to a building headquartered in Metropolis, the setting has popped up in Central City on the CW's *The Flash,* where an unfortunate incident gives the titular hero his superspeed.

The big-screen version of S.T.A.R. Labs has been introduced before. In *Man of Steel,* Richard Schiff played Dr. Emil Hamilton. (In the comics Hamilton is a S.T.A.R. researcher in several Superman stories.) And a corner of the facility

An early production-design conception of S.T.A.R. Labs.

Joe Morton as Dr. Silas Stone.

actually appeared for the first time in *Batman v Superman: Dawn of Justice*, in a brief found-footage file that revealed both Dr. Stone and his son Victor (Ray Fisher). In the footage, the doctor attempts to rescue his all-but-deceased son—with help from a mysterious black cube, referred to only as "U.S. Gov. Object 6-19-82."

We know now that this is, in fact, a Mother Box—an artifact that ties into the mysterious cosmic forces of Apokolips. Dr. Stone tampers with that technology for good reasons—but at what cost? "It's responsible for Cyborg's existence," says producer Charles Roven. "But it's also got consequences. It's not necessarily controllable by the person who's endowed with it." Good or bad, S.T.A.R.'s science is unquestionably mad.

Lost Action Hero

HE GAVE HIS LIFE TO PROTECT A WORLD THAT DIDN'T APPRECIATE HIS LOVE, AND HIS SACRIFICE HAS BECOME A SOURCE OF INSPIRATION FOR THE VERY PEOPLE WHO ONCE REFUSED HIM. NOW THE LAST SON OF KRYPTON HAS ONE FINAL STEP IN HIS CHRISTLIKE JOURNEY: RESURRECTION. *By Oliver Sava*

Superman, painted by comic artist Alex Ross.

SUPERMAN SAVES THE DAY. IT'S WHAT HE DOES.
But that doesn't necessarily mean he's everyone's favorite hero. When Zack Snyder's *Batman v Superman: Dawn of Justice* opens, for example, Henry Cavill's Kal-El is under fire from both the public and politicians for the widespread destruction he caused while battling the evil General Zod. Still, people need his help, and he won't allow bureaucracy to keep him from taking action. He's willing to give his life if it means mankind's salvation, and when a genetically engineered alien monster terrorizes the world, Superman makes the ultimate sacrifice in order to defeat it.

But as the saying goes, it's hard to keep a good man down. So, when it comes to the last son of Krypton, a hero who exemplifies the best of every human trait, you'd better believe he's not going to stay down for the count for long, Doomsday or no. Sure, Supes might have been dead and buried by the end of *Batman v Superman*, but the film's final image—the dirt above his coffin levitating—suggests there's something left to tell in his story.

The cycle of death and resurrection is a major aspect of many of the world's most revered religions and mythologies, and Snyder has been upfront about highlighting the character's Christian undertones ever since Cavill's debut in 2013's *Man of Steel*. He's the son of an otherworldly being, sent to Earth and taken in by a kindly childless couple, with superhuman abilities that inspire him to help others. Snyder showed the hero floating above Earth in a crucifixion pose and had Superman tempted by a Kryptonian villain who wants him to embrace his godly power and give up on humanity.

While numerous superhero stories have rejected the finality of death, Superman's demises, and his resurrections, tend to carry more weight simply because of his status as a towering comic-book icon. In his 79-year history, he's been killed off and brought back in multiple ways, events that have almost always coincided with either major changes to the character or to the larger DC Comics Universe.

It's a cycle seen with Alan Moore and Curt Swan's 1986 classic *Whatever Happened to the Man of Tomorrow?*—a two-parter concluding the story of the Superman that readers had been following for more than 20 years. At that time DC had plans to usher in a brand-new updated take on Superman as part of its *Crisis on Infinite Earths* miniseries, which was designed to condense a complicated continuity involving a multiverse of different Earths into one single universe.

Before the new Man of Steel debuted, however, DC Comics editor Julius Schwartz wanted to give the old Superman a proper goodbye that paid tribute to the decades of work that had been done with the character and his world.

Moore's story is far darker than what came before, and that change in tone was part of a shift that was gradually overtaking superhero comics. After his archnemesis Lex Luthor is slain, Superman kills himself by giving up his powers and walking out into the Arctic—according to a story Lois Elliott (née Lane) tells a reporter. While Superman and Clark Kent may be dead to the world, the man who

▲

Above and far left, top:
Henry Cavill as
Superman in *Batman v
Superman: Dawn of
Justice*. The 2016 film
ended with Superman
sacrificing his life to
stop Doomsday. Far left,
bottom: the Eternal
Flame that graces
Superman's grave.

◄

Batman v Superman
was loosely based
on the plot of the
bestselling 1993 comic
book *Superman #75*.

assumed those names is not. With a Burt Reynolds mustache and a brash new attitude, Jordan Elliott lives a quiet life with his wife and toddler son, and despite all the death and despair in this story, Superman and Lois get a happy ending.

The post-*Crisis* Superman was more vulnerable than his predecessor, which made the hero more relatable while opening up new storytelling possibilities. He would meet his end at the hands of the seemingly invincible villain Doomsday in 1992's *The Death of Superman*, a story that became a genuine pop-culture sensation. Dan Jurgens and Brett Breedings's *Superman #75* remains one of the bestselling comics of all time, and it served as the inspiration for the hero's demise in *Batman v Superman*.

New heroes like Superboy, Steel and Cyborg Superman were introduced before the original model was resurrected in 1993, and when Superman finally came back, he was sporting a mullet and all-black bodysuit with a gray S-shield. (The events of this story line would also directly feed into DC's 1994 continuity-shuffling event *Zero Hour: Crisis In Time*, which created a new singular timeline.)

This grimmer, more intense Superman was far more like the one Cavill plays onscreen. He would gradually lighten up in the years leading up to DC's 2011 New 52 event, which erased the previously existing versions of nearly every major character. It eliminated Superman's marriage to Lois Lane, putting him in a new relationship with Wonder Woman and outfitting him with a new costume that ditched the red briefs.

When this new interpretation failed to resonate with readers, DC killed off the New 52 Superman as part of its 2016 Rebirth event. Superman was replaced by the previous iteration, who had managed to escape the erasure of his universe and was living in secret with Lois and their son Jonathan (because comics). One Superman falls, another returns, and all of DC Comics undergoes a Rebirth soon afterward.

For now Superman's future is a mystery, but based on his comic-book history,

Above left: Superman and his superfamily from 2016's *Superman Rebirth*. Above right: Wonder Woman shares a moment with the superhero in *The New 52,* the DC Comics relaunch from 2011. Right: Cavill as Superman in *Batman v Superman: Dawn of Justice.*

> ❝It is no secret that I will be suited and booted (and caped) for Justice League at some point. What is the League without our big boy blue after all?❞
>
> —*Henry Cavill*

there's little doubt Superman will return once more. Cavill himself agrees. "One of the most exciting things about Superman's death in Zack Snyder's *Batman v Superman* is that it has provided a wonderful springboard for a chrysalis-like event," he says. "Who will we see emerge?"

Like his comic-book iterations, the big-screen Superman's death comes at a time of significant change: 2016 and 2017 saw major expansion for the DC movie lineup with the debuts of both 2016's *Suicide Squad* and 2017's *Wonder Woman*. Recent months have witnessed a raft of announcements about planned future films, including two centering on the Joker and Harley Quinn. Jason Momoa's stand-alone *Aquaman* is set for 2018; and in 2020 Ezra Miller will speed into theaters in his very own *Flashpoint*.

Will the return of Superman lead to a bright new day for the DC film universe? A new, fresh start for the character, perhaps taking his place at the head of the League, could help the mixed reception for the character in recent days—and according to recent reports, the DC filmmakers are giving their directors a bit more rein. For instance, Patty Jenkins's *Wonder Woman*'s more optimistic aesthetic won over audiences and critics to become the summer's biggest box office hit, and both Jenkins and Gal Gadot are back for the sequel in 2019. But it's 2017's *Justice League* that will determine the future path for DC's characters onscreen. Superman's death and resurrection could be the thing that helps steer this franchise away from the darkness and into the light.

ENTERTAINMENT WEEKLY
Editorial Director Jess Cagle
Editor Henry Goldblatt
Creative Director Tim Leong

JUSTICE LEAGUE
Editor Alyssa Smith
Editor, People + EW Books Allison Adato
Executive Editor Gina McIntyre
Designer Sung Choi
Photo Editor Robert Conway
Photo Editor, People + EW Books C. Tiffany Lee-Ramos
Writers Anthony Breznican, Darren Franich,
Caleb Goellner, Sean Howe,
John Jackson Miller, Noel Murray,
Oliver Sava, Nicole Sperling
Reporter Daniel S. Levy
Copy Desk Joanann Scali (Chief),
James Bradley (Deputy), Ellen Adamson,
Gabrielle Danchick, Richard Donnelly, Rose Kaplan,
Ben Harte, Matt Weingarden (Copy Editors)
Production Designer Peter Niceberg
Premedia Executive Director Richard Prue
Senior Manager Romeo Cifelli
Manager Rob Roszkowski
Imaging Production Associate
Franklin Abreu, Ana Kaljaj
Research Director Céline Wojtala

TIME INC. BOOKS
Publisher Margot Schupf
Vice President, Finance Cateryn Kiernan
Vice President, Marketing Jeremy Biloon
Executive Director, Marketing Services
Carol Pittard
Director, Brand Marketing Jean Kennedy
Sales Director Christi Crowley
Associate Director, Brand Marketing
Bryan Christian
Associate Director, Finance Jill Earyes
Assistant General Counsel Andrew Goldberg
Assistant Director, Production
Susan Chodakiewicz
Senior Manager, Finance Ashley Petrasovic
Brand Manager Katherine Barnet
Prepress Manager Alex Voznesenskiy
Associate Project and Production Manager
Anna Riego Muñiz

Editorial Director Kostya Kennedy
Creative Director Gary Stewart
Director of Photography Christina Lieberman
Editorial Operations Director Jamie Roth Major
Manager, Editorial Operations Gina Scauzillo
Associate Art Director Allie Adams
Copy Chief Rina Bander
Assistant Editor Courtney Mifsud

SPECIAL THANKS
Brad Beatson, Melissa Frankenberry, Kristina Jutzi,
Simon Keeble, Seniqua Koger, Kate Roncinske, Kristen Zwicker

Copyright 2017 Time Inc. Books

Published by Time Inc. Books
225 Liberty Street
New York, NY 10281

PHOTO CREDITS
COVER: Clay Enos/Warner Bros.; inset: DC Entertainment; **BACK COVER:** DC Entertainment; **Pg 1:** Warner Bros.; **Pg 2-3:** Warner Bros.; **Pg 6-7:** Warner Bros.; **Pg 8-9:** Clay Enos/Warner Bros. (2); Simmons: Warner Bros.; **Pg 10-11:** Clay Enos/Warner Bros. (3); **Pg 12-13:** Clay Enos/Warner Bros. (2); Warner Bros.; **Pg 14-15:** Warner Bros. (3); Miller: Clay Enos/Warner Bros.; **Pg 16-17:** Clay Enos/Warner Bros. (2); **Pg 18-19:** Clay Enos/Warner Bros.; Jonathan Prime/Warner Bros.; **Pg 20-21:** Matthias Clamer; **Pg 23:** Matthias Clamer; **Pg 24-25:** Cavill: Jamie McCarthy/WireImage; Matthias Clamer; **Pg 26-27:** Simmons: Warner Bros.; Nielsen: Clay Enos/Warner Bros.; Irons: Jonathan Prime/Warner Bros.; **Pg 28-29:** Jonathan Prime/Warner Bros. (2); Morton: Clay Enos/Warner Bros.; **Pg 30:** Carolyn Cole/LA Times/Contour by Getty Images; **Pg 31:** Clay Enos/Warner Bros. (3); **Pg 32:** Firefly: Snap Stills/REX/Shutterstock; Buffy: James Sorenson; Dr. Horrible: Amy Opoka; **Pg 33:** Art Streiber/August; **Pg 34-35:** Warner Bros. (2); **Pg 36-37:** Warner Bros. (2); **Pg 38-39:** Warner Bros. (3); **Pg 42-43:** DC Entertainment; **Pg 44-45:** DC Entertainment (5); **Pg 46-47:** DC Entertainment (6); **Pg 48-49:** DC Entertainment (4); **Pg 50:** Warner Bros.; **Pg 52:** DC Entertainment (2); **Pg 53:** Warner Bros.; **Pg 54:** Warner Bros.; **Pg 55:** DC Entertainment; **Pg 56-57:** Warner Bros. (3); **Pg 58:** Warner Bros.; **Pg 60:** DC Entertainment (2); **Pg 61:** Warner Bros.; **Pg 62:** Themyscira: Warner Bros.; Clay Enos/Warner Bros.; **Pg 63:** DC Entertainment; **Pg 64-65:** Amazonians: Clay Enos/Warner Bros.; Warner Bros. (2); **Pg 66:** Warner Bros.; **Pg 68:** DC Entertainment (3); **Pg 69:** Warner Bros.; **Pg 70:** DC Entertainment (3); **Pg 71:** Warner Bros.; **Pg 72-73:** Heard: Zack Snyder/Warner Bros.; Warner Bros.; **Pg 74:** Warner Bros.; **Pg 76:** DC Entertainment (2); **Pg 77:** Warner Bros.; **Pg 78:** DC Entertainment (3); Gustin: Diyah Pera/The CW; **Pg 79:** Warner Bros.; **Pg 80-81:** no costume: Clay Enos/Warner Bros.; Warner Bros. (2); **Pg 82:** Warner Bros.; **Pg 84:** DC Entertainment (2); **Pg 85:** Warner Bros.; **Pg 86:** Teen Titans: Warner Home Video; New Teen Titans: DC Entertainment; Smallville: Michael Courtney/The CW; **Pg 87:** Warner Bros.; **Pg 88-89:** Morton: Clay Enos/Warner Bros.; Warner Bros.; **Pg 90-91:** Alex Ross/DC Entertainment; **Pg 92-93:** tomb: Clay Enos/Warner Bros.; Death Of Superman: DC Entertainment; Warner Bros. (2); **Pg 94:** DC Entertainment (2); **Pg 95:** Clay Enos/Warner Bros.; **Pg 96:** 1,f: shopdcentertainment.com; 4,d: Clay Enos/Warner Bros. (2); 8: DC Entertainment; a: Zade Rosenthal/Warner Bros.; b: Hulton Archive/Getty Images; c: Ron Phillips/Warner Bros.; e,g,h: paulmartstore.com (3)

TEST YOUR SUPERHERO IQ!

How well do you know the League?
We go back to the team's 1960 origins to see how you've
kept up. **BY ALYSSA SMITH**

1. The Justice League, pictured here in action figurines inspired by the film (now available from JAKKS Pacific), was founded in 1960. Which two heroes from the original lineup are missing? (**Bonus question:** Which hero joined the team with the 2011 comic-book reboot?)

2. The Rogues are the supervillain group facing off against which member of the Justice League?

3. Which villain is responsible for the death of Bruce Wayne's parents?

4. Aquaman sets up new headquarters for the team in which Great Lakes-adjacent city in 1984?

5. Who is Diana's aunt?

6. Which character was created with the powers and skills of the entire Justice League?

7. Match Batman to his Batmobile.

8. What was the original print run of *Superman #75*, in which Superman meets his end at the hands of Doomsday?

9. Who was the first villain to fight the assembled League?

10. Name the original teen sidekick of the 1960 team.

11. Who are the two creators of Superman?

12. After the DC event *Crisis*, which heroine replaced Wonder Woman as a founding member?

13. Put these iterations of the Flash in order of comicbook appearances:
○ **Barry Allen**
○ **Johnny Quick**
○ **Wally West**
○ **Jay Garrick**

★ ★ ★ ★ **14.** FINISH THE LINE: "IN BRIGHTEST DAY, IN BLACKEST NIGHT,..." ★ ★ ★ ★

Printed in Great Britain
by Amazon